THE
NEBRASKA
WINTER
OF 1948–49

THE
NEBRASKA
WINTER
OF 1948–49

STORIES OF SURVIVAL

BARRY D. SEEGEBARTH

THE
History
PRESS

Published by The History Press
Charleston, SC
www.historypress.com

First published 2023

Manufactured in the United States

ISBN 9781467154239

Library of Congress Control Number: 2023937206

To my late grandmother Celia Seegebarth for instilling in me an interest in and appreciation of history.

CONTENTS

ACKNOWLEDGEMENTS

There are several people and organizations I would like to thank, because without their help, this book would not have been possible. Thank you to Lindsey Hillgartner and the reference staff at History Nebraska; Libby McKay and Drew DeCamp at the Elkhorn Valley Museum in Norfolk; Vickie DeJong at the Pierce Nebraska Historical Society; and Cheri Schrader at the Platte County Historical Society for the use of your photographs. Thank you to Gerald Hixson of Pierce for taking the time to meet with me and for the use of your personal photographs. Thank you to the *Pierce County Leader*, the *Norfolk Daily News*, the *Omaha World-Herald* and the *Lincoln Journal Star*. Also, thank you to the Norfolk Public Library for use of your digitized newspaper archives. Thank you to my editor, Chad Rhoad, at The History Press. To Betty Mapes, Crystal Werger and Ellen Mortensen, thank you for your assistance. I would also like to thank my father, Doug Seegebarth of Hadar; my aunt JoAnn Winter of Norfolk; and, most important of all, my wife, Janet Seegebarth.

INTRODUCTION

I t was the story your grandparents never stopped talking about, a period recalled with more frequency than maybe the Great Depression and World War II. It was the winter of 1948–49, a season of weather so severe that even the people who lived through it, people thoroughly accustomed to bitter Nebraska winters, will never forget.

This was a winter of brutal cold, unbearable winds and record snowfall, sometimes making streets and highways impassable and travel by foot, horse, car or train impossible. It was, at worst, a time of snowbound farmers and ranchers facing deadly cold and hunger because their supply of coal and food had run out, only to be saved in the nick of time with supplies delivered by plane. It was, at best, months of sheer boredom for people trying to pass the time and maintain their fragile sanity after the cancelation of events like weddings, sports and family gatherings due to the impossibility of travel.

It was a winter that stubbornly refused to end. The winter of 1948–49 was so severe that the governor of Nebraska had to request the federal government to send the air force to air-drop bales of hay to starving cattle in the open country. This period contained tales of tragedy, like when citizens' cars were stalled on a highway and they were forced to walk the rest of the way home, only to get lost and freeze to death from exposure to deadly windchill or literally suffocate and drown in the hurricane-force winds that drove snow into their noses and throats.

This snowy season forced many city, county and state highway councils to redesign and rebuild their highways by raising them up and providing side medians and snow fences to prevent snowbanks from drifting over the top of them. Budgeting started for the purchase of snowplows along with deicing salt and chemicals to clear highways of the elements. The science of weather forecasting was improved on, as was the study of the formation and movement of winter storms to better warn the general public before the flurries arrived in the area. That winter mocked us with snowbanks that survived in ditches until late May; there were even patches of ice that remained in the shade of tree groves until the Fourth of July.

If there is one thing that Nebraskans obsess about—other than politics, football and crops—it is the weather. Every year, the citizens of this state eagerly await the publication of the annual *Old Farmer's Almanac* in the fall, which contains the coming winter forecast, just as fanatically as some people read their daily horoscope, whether it is accurate or not. With foreboding dread, they nervously watch their local television weather segment about the arrival of a severe winter storm and decide how much earlier in the morning they should leave for work. Or if the roads are bad enough, they may refuse to travel to work at all.

Every Nebraskan has tales of white-knuckle driving on a slick ice- or snow-covered street, trying to keep their vehicle from sliding into a ditch or into oncoming traffic, sometimes successfully and occasionally resulting in a head-on collision. They know the frustration of running late for work on a cold winter morning, scampering out to their car that is sitting outside, only to be greeted with their windows crusted over with a sheet of frost that has to be frantically removed by hand with a window scraper. They remember being grade school kids and waking up in the morning to the glorious news from their mother that school had been canceled and that they could spend the rest of the day doing what every kid desired: the important things in life, like watching cartoons, wasting hours playing video games or having their noses buried in a comic book.

With that in mind, the worst winter of all, the winter of 1948–49, would leave an indelible, unforgettable imprint on the memories of those who survived it. Imagine the heartbreak of having to burn an old family heirloom for firewood, just to provide warmth for the day because the coal had ran out. Picture what it must have been like for the man of the farmhouse to leave his wife and kids alone to trudge through snow-buried fields by foot to get to town to buy vital supplies and not know if he would make it back. Or envision the melancholy of learning that a neighbor, someone who had just been seen and talked to the day before, had slipped and fallen on a patch of ice on her porch steps, hit her head on the pavement and died from a brain hemorrhage.

A woman posing in front of a snow-covered house. Snowdrifts this winter reached as high as thirty feet. *History Nebraska.*

This cruel, unforgiving winter also had its enjoyable—although painfully overdue—conclusion. Imagine the sheer ecstasy of seeing the snow finally start to melt, exposing the green grasses that had been hidden for far too long by a deep, white shroud or the joy of being able to walk outside without the cold, arctic air stinging you in the face. After being cooped up for far too long, people were delighted by the smell of the fresh, moist air evaporating from the ground, filling their noses and lungs with nourishment, and the contentment of knowing that when the winter was finally over, they would be able to live life like normal people again—at least until next winter.

These sights, stories and emotions are what you will find in the following pages of this book, which tries to capture on paper all the hardships so many citizens of Nebraska had to endure at that time. Reading about an experience is not the same as living it, but the least we can do is remember these events and pass on to future generations the lessons learned during those months. I hope you enjoy reading this book as thoroughly as I enjoyed writing it.

1

NO ONE SAW IT COMING

During a very mild fall and harvest season in the state of Nebraska, nothing led anyone to suspect the upcoming onslaught of severe weather during the winter of 1948–49. In the couple of months prior, conditions in the Cornhusker State were warmer and dryer than usual, leading to a relatively easy picking season and a bountiful harvest. Temperate air in October and early November allowed many people to wear short sleeves when doing outdoor work and to play in almost summer-like conditions.

Unfortunately, what made this winter so devastating—in addition to the heavy snowfall—was the primitive state of the science of weather forecasting compared to the computerized, mega-data-driven methods employed today. At the time, there were no satellites, weather radars or supercomputers. Curiosities such as the jet stream and upper atmospheric conditions had been recently discovered during World War II from the first flights of ballistic missiles and high-altitude bombers. Reports from America's towns to the Weather Bureau's regional offices were literally "phoned in" or teletyped by human observers. This information was, in turn, distributed to the public via newspapers, radio or large billboards displayed inside public buildings, like hotel lobbies and train stations.[1] Most importantly, weather reporting agencies did not do long-term, extended forecasts. There was, of course, the *Old Farmer's Almanac*, but that was more of an unscientific "guesstimate" as to what the coming winter would bring.

A helicopter parked in front of the Norfolk Airport. The airport housed the local weather bureau. *Elkhorn Valley Museum.*

In fact, there was a strong prejudice against meteorologists who even *attempted* to predict weather patterns more than a week in advance. It was a practice considered akin to fortune telling. Weather bureaus were much more concerned with reports from citizens about the *current* weather conditions of a certain area than in what *might* happen the next day or the next week. Weather conditions contain millions of variables, like temperature, humidity, wind speed and direction; not even thousands of mathematicians monitoring the same storm with slide rulers could figure out how big a particular storm would get, what direction it would travel in and how much precipitation it would drop on a particular area, whether it was over a square mile, a town or an entire state or region. It would take the very recent invention of the electronic computer, with its vacuum tubes, gigantic size that filled entire rooms and ability to calculate millions of equations per second, for the public to finally get some reliable weather forecasting, but that would not come to pass for several more years.[2]

Another problem Nebraska faced in winter was its shortage of reliable snowplows. They were adequate when it came to mild or average winter seasons, but they were woefully lacking during harsh times, as many cities and towns were about to find out when this winter began. Most of the snowplows and bulldozers in Nebraska were at least ten or fifteen years old, and many were in poor condition. This was because of World War II. The U.S. military took priority when it came to industry supplying the newest bulldozers, snowplows and other snow and ice removal equipment. Last but not least was the primitive state of early highway construction and maintenance. Roads, especially gravel ones in the country, were built flush to the ground, making them susceptible to snow drifting over them, unlike modern roads, which have raised bodies.

2

WINTER'S FIRST STRIKE

Monday, November 15, started out like a mild, summer day: clear, with temperatures in the seventies and a gentle southern breeze. But like a con artist deceiving his mark, this day once again added to Nebraska's infamous reputation for extreme weather and its ability to swing rapidly in the opposite direction. People began their day going to work or school and running errands without a care in the world. Everything seemed a little too perfect. Then, in the late afternoon, the wind changed directions to the north and northwest, bringing cooler air with it.

After nightfall, a slight sprinkling of rain began to dribble on the occupants below, indicating a change in the weather was coming. By daybreak the next morning, the rain had intensified into a torrent, with much stronger wind gusts driving it diagonally on its way to the ground. After sunset, the rain turned to sleet and ice, causing roadways and sidewalks to become treacherously slick for cars and pedestrians. After midnight on Wednesday, the ice storm exploded into a full-scale blizzard, complete with all the trappings of a Midwest snowstorm: heavy snowfall, zero visibility, near-hurricane-force winds and deadly wind chills.[3]

Long-distance travelers who were unlucky enough to be caught on the open highway scrambled to reach the nearest farmhouse in the hopes they would find a sympathetic resident willing to give them a bed or even a carpeted floor to sleep on. Some motorists who were fortunate enough to inch their way to the nearest town came to their senses and quit while they were ahead, seeking refuge wherever they could find it, be it in an open church or at the residence of a friendly citizen offering shelter for the night.

Main Street in Pierce. Many stranded travelers relied on the kindness of strangers to give them food and lodging. *Pierce Nebraska Historical Society.*

Others did not heed the advice of locals to quit while they were ahead and spend the night at a motel or on a stranger's couch. Some decided instead to throw caution to the wind—literally—and press on to their final destination, be it Lincoln, Omaha or farther, regardless of the fact they could not see past the hood of their vehicle and were fishtailing on the highway, coming precariously close to the ditch.

Some people were not so lucky. Their vehicles slid into ditches or directly into the paths of impassible snowdrifts. Those with enough gas in their tanks were able to run their engines through the night, keeping hot air flowing through the heating vents and maintaining a life-sustaining temperature. Others, whose tanks ran dry or did not have the minimum cold weather clothing, like stocking caps, gloves and insulated snow boots, had to resort to extreme measures like ripping the foam out of their seat cushions and molding it into makeshift garments they could put their hands and feet into, saving them from frostbite.

Those who did manage to find lodging and a place to rest had to deal with the dilemma of eating. Hotels that normally did their slowest business in the

The first blizzard hit on November 18. Some were able to reach their Thanksgiving destinations, but others were not so lucky. *Pierce Nebraska Historical Society.*

winter, with mostly vacant rooms, now had to deal with double and even triple capacity. Overwhelmed staff had to cope with hungry and irate customers and scare up whatever morsels they could find, be it canned vegetables in the basement or a giant kettle of chicken noodle soup brewed for easy and quick nourishment for a large number of people. Lack of privacy and space was the price to pay for such unexpected accommodations, but it sure beat freezing to death in the open country.

By Sunday, the snow had stopped, and stranded motorists began to leave their meager accommodations, get back inside their vehicles, gas up and continue on their journeys. Local authorities began directing snowplows where they were needed and punching holes through the nearly impassable snowdrifts that seemed to block every possible avenue of escape out of their towns. Some people were able to continue to their Thanksgiving destinations. Others became travel shy and decided to leave well enough alone and stay put where they were.

Main Street in Pierce. Front-loading tractors were indispensable machines in the ongoing fight against the snowbanks. *Elkhorn Valley Museum.*

Main Street in Pierce. Many businesses took a hit financially or closed temporarily during the winter of 1948–49. *Elkhorn Valley Museum.*

When the snow mercifully ended on Saturday, November 20, the region tallied up the damages. Residents and weathermen alike proclaimed this was probably the worst November snowstorm the state had ever experienced. It had followed a roughly southwest to northeast path from McCook through Grand Island and into Hartington. McCook received almost a foot of snow, while central Nebraska towns like Burwell and Albion received around a foot and a half. The biggest wallop of the storm hit northeast Nebraska, where the towns of Creighton, Wausa, Bloomfield and Hartington received as much as twenty to twenty-four inches of snow, aided in no small part thanks to the extra moisture evaporated from the Missouri River, which ran in between Nebraska and South Dakota.[4]

The "Old Muddy," as many in the area nicknamed the Missouri River, is actually the longest river in America, and throughout its history, anytime a low-pressure system crossed it in the winter, it basically produced lake-effect snow for the area, transforming minor snow events into gargantuan droppings of frozen precipitation. Areas northwest and southwest of the roughly diagonal path of the storm were left relatively unscathed. Valentine, located in the north-central part of the state, received only a dusting, while Omaha, Nebraska's largest city on its eastern border with Iowa, straddling the Missouri River, received only rain, sleet and a snowy mix.

The storm would eventually barrel into southeastern South Dakota, northwestern Iowa and southwestern Minnesota in a roughly diagonal, northeasterly direction. Many telephone and telegraph lines were broken, making towns and newspapers dependent on radio for outside information.[5]

In an ironic twist of technological fate, rural farmhouses that still did not have electrical service even in normal times and good weather had the enviable luck of being able to stay warm with coal and wood stoves, while some of their city neighbors, dependent on electrical furnaces, suffered from the cold. Occupants of homes with old-fashioned heating systems who had a heart took mercy on their unfortunate neighbors by letting them stay for a day or two until their power was restored.

The *Pierce County Leader*, in its November 25, 1948 edition, reported this as "one of the heaviest snowstorms ever to strike this early in the year.… Over seven inches of snow fell, piling into drifts ten and twelve feet deep on main street."[6]

After having very nice temperatures on November 15, the people in Pierce County were not prepared for the rain that turned to snow on Thursday, November 18. Visitors swiftly became snowbound, and farmers could not

Those in rural areas who did not have electricity were in good shape, as they were well-stocked with fuel for heating. *Elkhorn Valley Museum.*

This photograph shows Main Street in Pierce. The main street of any town always had first priority when it came to snow removal. *Elkhorn Valley Museum.*

make their way home and had to stay in town. Although the people in Pierce did not lose electricity, the snow and the wind that started as light rain on Thursday raged throughout the night and continued all day on Friday. Most of the area's businesses and schools closed, and the mail delivery trucks did not even make it to Pierce.

The people of Nebraska have negotiated many days and nights of heavy snow and blowing winds, but this was one of the worst, with wind gusts reaching speeds of seventy-six miles per hour and temperatures staying below freezing, dipping to just nine degrees Fahrenheit on Sunday night.

The *Pierce County Leader* continued: "One of the most unusual features of the blizzard was the vivid lightning and accompanying thunder which continued until 1:00 Friday morning. Lightning struck WJAG at Norfolk further cutting Pierce off from the surrounding towns. Repairs were not completed until 4:00 Friday afternoon."[7]

On Saturday morning, all those available in town took up their shovels and began digging out the entryways to the downtown businesses. As is the custom in many small towns like Pierce, free coffee and donuts were served to anyone who volunteered to help. Many snow shovels were furiously digging paths around the farms as well.

From Saturday to Wednesday, blades pushed the snow and cleared more and more streets in the town. Schools actually reopened on Monday, but many of the rural students were absent, as some of the roads were still impassable with drifts too deep and dangerous to attempt transporting children to and from school. Many of the stores began to reopen after the weekend, but it was not until Tuesday night that the plows finally stopped, and the snow hauling was over. The streets were considered clear enough for automobiles to get around again.

From the *Pierce County Leader*: "The citizens of Pierce and city officials are very appreciative of the cooperation and assistance extended them by the operators of the two snow loaders, the truckers and scoopers on the unloading line at the Gilman Park. Without their help Pierce would have been in a bad way as far as snow problems are concerned."[8]

Another article from the *Pierce County Leader* read as follows: "Farmers with no exceptions (we feel safe in saying) have had to learn to cope with an early, extremely difficult winter which set in to stay following nearly a week of lovely, balmy weather through the middle of November."[9]

Because of the nice weather during the earlier fall months, most of the farmers in the area had already harvested their corn before this storm hit, but there were a few acres of corn still waiting to be picked. How strange

This hayrack is being pulled through the snow by a tractor outside of a farm in rural Nebraska. *Elkhorn Valley Museum.*

it must have seemed to these farmers to find drifts of snow the next day, some as deep as ten feet, after hearing thunder and seeing lightning and expecting rain.

The *Leader* reported:

> *Word came through November 22nd that it was possible to get to Pierce via Foster from Leo W. Krueger's without great difficulty. Krueger's reside on the Anton Turek Sr. farm. With the boys and girls from this territory who attend schools in Pierce snowbound, it was imperative to endeavor to make the trip. Pupils from this community include Virginia and George Prince; Hilda, Ann and Max Unseld, Jr.; Ruth Dean; Dennis Acklie; Dorothy, Lillian, Kathryn, Don and Kathleen Hoffmann; Janelle Rahl; Joann and Lois Ann Buss; Richard and LeRoy Fischer; Billy and Delores Stonacek; Melvin and Raymond Krueger; and Nelson Parks.*[10]

Those in the rural communities who thought the children should try to go to school on Tuesday traveled together, with tractors, cars and teams making up their caravan. Their intentions were good and their determination was strong, but after four hours of traveling, they had progressed only two miles.

Joyce, Betty and Leroy Sporleder at their farm west of Pierce. Children often learned to cope with the snowy conditions better than the adults did. *Gerald Hixson.*

Once they reached a main road, the last fifteen miles into Pierce still took another hour.

The *Leader* continued: "Our first mail delivery came through on November 29th, eleven days after that first blizzard. Carriers have been working very faithfully despite severe handicaps to deliver mail when and where they can possibly go."[11]

On December 3, with the road south of Mr. and Mrs. Leo Keller still being blocked, the community gathered for a charivari party. A cheerful group of around fifty people showed up from the east, west and north to congratulate and welcome the bride and groom. When the snowplow crew showed up later that evening to clear the southern route, they were treated to a warm welcome by the crowd of well-wishers.

The wind was not about to give up its severity. December 5 brought more of the same severe weather. "Mr. and Mrs. Norris Harding and their two small children of Norfolk had spent the previous night with her mother, Mrs. Ruth Walton, and her brother, Harold. By 7:30 am Monday they were on their way to return to their home. Mrs. Harding laughingly remarked to her mother, 'I don't have too much to worry about as I have a mechanic for a husband.'"[12]

Alois Hoffman had the idea that she would bring her three daughters to Pierce to stay with the Cary Dean family through the week so the children could attend school without the need to drive back and forth from their rural home. When they were still three miles outside of Pierce, by the old golf course, the family got stuck on a hill. Mr. Hoffman was determined to get into town and believed he could do it if he could just get over this hill. He got out his shovel and began digging their car out.

Before the family pressed on to try to make it to town, Mrs. Hoffman saw what looked like a car buried in the snow ahead. Upon inspection, it turned out that it was an abandoned car. The family gave up their idea to get over the hill and continue their trip into Pierce when they saw the car engulfed by the snowbank.

They then turned around and made it back to the Palmer Peterson farm. Here, they found the Harding family, who owned the abandoned car. They had been stranded and were staying with the Petersons until they were able to continue their journey.[13] Many people found themselves unable to reach their destinations that winter or with unexpected guests until things cleared up a bit.

Eventually, the thaw came, melting away snowdrifts and snow piles. But with the thaw came a new mess: a morass of flooded streets and sidewalks by day and slick, icy pavement by night. Muddy country roads made travel by automobile and tractor treacherous, so loading a pickup or farm vehicle with some chains on the tires and some extra weight in the back was a necessity if a driver wanted any traction at all.

Two men pause by a snowbank. Due to cold temperatures and blowing snow, much of the winter was spent repeatedly digging out roads. *Gerald Hixson.*

The citizens of Nebraska were hoping this unusually severe November blizzard was just an aberration, a freak tantrum of nature, and not a bad omen of what may lie ahead. Mercifully, more conventional weather arrived just in time for Thanksgiving weekend and early December, which allowed people to travel for family get-togethers and enjoy eating the foods of a bountiful harvest. Shortly thereafter, however, winter reared its ugly head again in the Cornhusker State, with a couple weeks of unsettled weather across the area. High wind storms in the panhandle around December 19 and 20 produced dust clouds almost as large as those of the Dust Bowl in the 1930s.[14] In other areas, snow showers produced anywhere from a couple inches to a foot and a half of the white stuff, and for good measure, some localities saw a mix of sleet and freezing drizzle.

Christmas was approaching by this time, and most were hoping that the November storms would be cleared up in time to celebrate the holidays. That was not to be the case, however, because heavy snow fell all day on December 23 and Christmas Eve. Then the wind picked up again. The Dean family had relatives who lived only half a mile down the road, but the roads were blocked. With determination, they did make Christmas that

Betty Sporleder stands by a hog barn west of Pierce. The second storm brought more snow to the area on December 28. *Gerald Hixson.*

year, but it took them nearly forty-five minutes to make it that half a mile to their destination.[15]

Another blizzard on December 28 followed almost the exact same path as the storm in November, moving once again in a diagonal southwest to northeast direction. This blizzard dumped anywhere from a foot to two feet of snow, causing sporadic power outages, workplace closures and event cancelations. This new storm was not quite as severe as its November counterpart, but it did leave considerable damage in its wake. Mercifully, the freezing temperatures of this period only lasted a couple of days and then swung back up to the thirties. This minimized livestock deaths and prevented wholesale losses of entire herds.[16]

These first six weeks of snowfall were enough to fill an entire normal winter season, but as fate would have it, Old Man Winter was just getting started. Nothing would compare to the arctic nightmare that would come to pass after the first of the year in 1949. The next three months would test the limits of machinery, natural resources and human endurance. Even the tough-skinned Nebraskans who were accustomed to brutal winters would have their resolves stretched to the breaking point. Some ranchers would lose their entire fortunes and life savings, some truckers would wreck their rigs in blinding blizzards and some would even pay with their lives.

3

THE BIGGEST BLIZZARD

S aturday, New Year's Day 1949, started off as the third week of the previous November had, like a case of déjà vu. The weather was unseasonably mild for that time of the year in Nebraska, almost spring-like, producing a merciful thaw for the Cornhusker State and giving false hope that the worst of winter's fury was behind them.

The next day, many Nebraskans went to church on a morning with mild temperatures and clear skies, but when they returned home to their Sunday dinner, they noticed a wall of dark gray clouds approaching from the west, increasing winds and a rapid drop in temperatures. Any midwesterner knew what was coming next. This was the start of a blizzard that would go down as one of the worst in the history of Nebraska.

It started as a massive low-pressure system in Colorado, moved easterly to Oklahoma and then took a sharp turn northward through Kansas, Nebraska and the Dakotas. Almost hurricane-like in its size and intensity, the storm pulled massive amounts of moisture in from the Gulf Coast and collided with an equally massive arctic cold front from Canada.[17] These two immovable forces stalled over the upper Midwest, producing a blizzard unequaled by any in Nebraska history, even the Children's Blizzard of 1888.

The disturbance hit the panhandle around late morning, the north-central part of the state by midafternoon and eastern Nebraska by sundown, bringing gale-force winds and what started out as flurries but then rapidly intensified into blindingly heavy snowfall, producing zero visibility and whiteout conditions. What separated this blizzard from others in Nebraska

A person climbs a snowbank by a newly plowed road. Children had plenty of snow days when roads were nearly impossible to traverse. *Gerald Hixson.*

history was its near hurricane-force winds, with average wind speeds around fifty miles per hour and some gusts with speeds recorded as high as seventy to eighty miles per hour.[18] This piled up drifts as tall as twenty to thirty feet, nearly burying many farmhouses in a snowy tomb.

Another harsh feature of this storm was that the snow particles in particular were of a hard, granular type, packing snowdrifts into what felt like the hardness of concrete, making digging out by shovel nearly impossible. If that was not bad enough, people who were unlucky enough to have to walk in this snowy hell faced the threat of not only frostbite but also suffocating from the inhalation of snow particles. In effect, they were under threat of drowning in the wind-driven snow. People tried all manner of solutions to combat this. Some used the old-fashioned, tried and true scarf wrapped around the mouth and nose method or walking backward. Others used the unique solution of holding a shovel in front of their face while they walked. World War II veteran pilots who kept their old oxygen masks used them as protection from the wind.

JoAnn Winter (formerly JoAnn Seegebarth) remembered this storm quite well. As a child living in northeast Nebraska, she walked early Monday morning with some difficulty to her one-room country school from her farm outside of Hadar, making it there safely. Knowing the walk after school would not be any better, she and her fellow classmates, as well as their teacher, prayed for improved conditions by midafternoon so they would not have to spend the night sleeping on the cold, hard wooden floors. But that was not to be the case. The weather had deteriorated by noon, forcing the young occupants to hunker down for the evening.

The teacher rationed the food students had brought for lunch so they would have enough to last until the first light of the morning. JoAnn's father, Delbert Seegebarth, had enough to worry about back at the farm with cattle he was trying to keep from freezing to death. Now, he had to worry about his daughter trying to walk home in a blinding blizzard. Thankfully, because of the cautious decisions of the schoolteacher, a tragedy was avoided, and the children walked home safely the next morning.[19]

When the storm mercifully ended on Wednesday, January 5, the final snow totals were hard to believe. Amounts varied greatly from town to town, as the storm had produced between ten and twenty-five inches of snow. But the unlucky champion of this latest storm was Chadron in the northwest corner of Nebraska, which was the recipient of an outrageous amount of forty inches of snow.[20] This king of the blizzards caught many Nebraskans by surprise. The state newspapers gave the United States Weather Bureau a tongue lashing in the next few days, saying fishboat captains and birds could give better weather predictions than the mutimillion-dollar federal agency.

What separated this new phase of winter from the rest was the arrival of constant, bitterly cold arctic air and winds. After this latest blizzard, the frigid air kept the snow cover in a constant powdery state, allowing for the continuous drifting of snow without any additional precipitation. Snowplow crews around the state would often dig out a road in the morning, only to have it drift back shut by nightfall.

Various small towns around the state came up with the novel solution of having their local radio station announce that their country roads into town were freshly plowed. Hearing this, nearby residents who lived on farms would scurry into town as quickly as possible, buy their precious supplies and scurry back home before new drifting could trap them. For snow removal crews, it was like a cruel game of winter whack-a-mole. Bulldozer and maintainer drivers would toil for hours on end, pushing snow off a highway or gravel road, only to have it be completely snow-packed again in a day or two, like they did not even do the job the first, second or third time.

Little did anyone know that the heavy snow and high winds experienced in November and December were far from over. "Weatherwise 1949 got

A man, his dog and his car are flanked by two snowbanks in Holt County, near the H.R. Holcomb farm. *History Nebraska.*

off to a wild start in Nebraska," said Ralph Smith in the January 1949 *Omaha World-Herald* article titled "Oklahoma Blew Storm Our Way."[21] Since thousands of *Omaha World-Herald* readers did not receive a paper for many days during the bad weather, the newspaper decided to print a special section to keep their readers updated.

The article reported: "New Year's Day was clear and pleasant. Temperatures throughout the state smacked of late autumn. Sidney and Scottsbluff had highs of 40, Chadron of 38, North Platte 37, Lincoln 32. Omaha and Grand Island, with readings of 29 and 27, alone reported below freezing temperatures."[22]

Milder weather continued into January 2, and the Nebraska forecast had indicated that it would be a cloudy day with some light snow and a high around thirty degrees. However, the prospects of a mild January were struck down. A storm was brewing in Oklahoma that would soon reach Kansas and then Nebraska.

The storm was reported as almost hurricane-like in nature, with the center of it calm and clear. The whipping winds revolved like a cyclone, bringing wind gusts up to sixty-five miles per hour. The more southern areas received milder temperatures and rain, while the northern areas were active with arctic air and blowing snow that created yet another round of low visibility and high snowdrifts. After traveling through Colorado and Wyoming, the

A large snowbank spreads across the front of this house. Many people felt like they were buried alive this winter. *History Nebraska.*

storm hit the western part of Nebraska first. The rest of Nebraska could only prepare and wait for what was coming their way.

While those in Omaha considered themselves lucky to have missed the brunt of the January storm, some areas in western and central Nebraska, in a meteorological oddity, were hit by the same storm twice. As though changing its mind on where it wanted to dump its vast amounts of snow, the storm traveled north past Grand Island. It took a northwestern route over to Valentine and then doubled back on itself, curving around to exit the state to the northeast.

Once again, people in certain areas of Nebraska found themselves buried alive, with those stranded looking for places to stay and the sick and injured unable to reach medical facilities. Trains were unable to move, and supplies were running low. As is true today, transportation was a vital link between communities, especially in the rural areas of Nebraska in 1949. Basically, everyone was stuck where they were.

The huge amount of snow that fell this winter is a story in itself, but the other part of that story is how Nebraskans displayed their true nature by responding to the difficulties that arose during these blizzards. In Ogallala, with a population of 3,159, hotels and roadside homes were flooded with around 2,000 stranded travelers.[23] Agencies were set up in the community to offer even more places to stay; the goal was to find a bed for every person. They did their best to contribute whatever resources they could as more people sought shelter from the raging storm. The community was in this together, and they continued to do what they could to make their guests comfortable.

As word got out that sick people needed help, neighbors took up shovels and used their tractors to clear paths to help rescue them. Pilots took off on mercy flights to try to reach those who needed medical supplies. Sometimes, they would use skis to land so they could transport people to the hospital. Communications were slow, but individuals worked together as best as they could to develop coordinated plans. When a job was too much for a person to handle, entire neighborhoods turned out to pitch in and help wherever they could. Fuel-short communities shared and rationed what they had to keep everyone afloat until the devastation of the storm subsided.

Individuals and communities coordinated their efforts to help each other and do what they could to get through this predicament, but it soon became clear that even more help was needed. Smith said, "As the job proved too

Leroy Sporleder stands on a brooder house. Trails were more useful if they followed the tops of snowdrifts instead of the roads. *Gerald Hixson.*

great for local efforts, the organized agencies moved in. The Civil Air Patrol systematized rescue work over whole areas. The Red Cross came to back up scanty resources. The army came from Lowry Field and Kearney to carry loads beyond the ability of light local planes to tote."[24]

Handling this emergency situation took a lot of thought and planning from Governor Val Peterson. He coordinated efforts statewide by organizing all state departments to work with county sheriffs and an emergency flight crew from the Tenth Air Force at Indianapolis. The blizzard affected everyone: railroads, farmers, marooned travelers, snowbound ranchers, highway workers and isolated communities. The winter proved to be full of challenges, but it also brought out the best in people.

The 2,000 snow-locked people in Ogallala began to wonder where the snowplows were as they impatiently waited for them to show up and clear their road that went east and west, but the state highway department was stretched to its limit. The sheer amount of snow that needed to be moved was tremendous and slowed the department's work. Another 230 passengers from a Union Pacific train were marooned in Kimball. When they ran out of bread, the chefs from the dining cars fired up the ovens in order to make more. Supplies everywhere were running short.

Frank Stempek of Duncan led by the Challenger locomotive works to free a snowbound Union Pacific Railroad train. *Platte County Historical Society.*

According to Smith, "Wedge plows were virtually useless; only rotaries could handle the job. The department manned all it had, bought others and rented still more. Wyoming's highway department moved into northwest Nebraska with a lift. Even the rotaries had trouble coping with the snow, packed to the density of ice."[25]

Just keeping the snowplows running was a difficult task. When new rotaries arrived, they were out of service within a few hours due to the snow's stubborn icy hardness. The snow was so deep that crews had to resort to using dynamite to blast a path through it. The main highways were the first to be cleared, leaving rural areas and smaller towns to do what they could on their own.

Northwest Nebraska was the last area to finally receive help from the snowplows. Scottsbluff was not sure if its food and fuel supplies were going to last until transportation was available once again, so it, along with some of the smaller towns to the east, including Merriman, Gordon and Chadron, carefully evaluated their food supplies and weighed the amount of their provisions against the time left until the roads were opened.

They were running out of everything from fresh fruits to baby food and anything in between. Even dairies could not get their produce to the stores. One farmer, after filling all of his containers, decided to fill his bathtub with excess cream so it would not go to waste. Bread trucks did not deliver, so many households resurrected the art of bread making—that is if they could get ahold of the yeast needed.

People were stranded at home and away from home. Ranchers waited in the quiet for the sound of an approaching airplane, hoping the plane would see their message left stamped in the snow, written with coal or lumber or pegged with a quilt. Country phones buzzed with news of people who needed help or were sick. It was not unusual for a man, with strong determination, to go out with a shovel to dig and dig, but he would often clear no more than half a mile in over twenty-four hours.

For those unlucky enough to be trapped in their car for the duration of this storm, it was terrifying when the gas ran out and the motor died. Some lived to tell the tale, although they may have survived the bitter cold only to have their flesh damaged from frostbite. A couple trapped near Scottsbluff found a field of corn and managed to live off of that for three days until help arrived.

In Hay Springs, a father carried his eighteen-month-old baby and his unconscious wife through the storm until he found shelter a quarter of a mile down the road. Although the distance was not far, it took the man two

A snowdrift covers the front of this farmhouse. Shoveling snow and digging out was something that had to be done daily. *History Nebraska.*

hours to complete the task. The poor baby was so badly frostbitten by then that skin grafts were needed, but at least the family survived.

Others were not so lucky. A truck driver who got stuck near Ogallala decided to walk for help. The swirling snow and wind blocked his view, and he never saw the house that was about one hundred yards away. Another trucker also could not sit still. He died near the town of Harrison. If only he had noticed the haystack that was a few feet away, the protection it offered might have saved his life.[26]

Harold Cowan, a photographer-reporter with the *Omaha World-Herald*, was on the scene and wrote an article about the blizzard of January 2–4, 1949, called "Deep Misery for Man with Mile-Wide Appetite."[27] From Omaha, he drove as far west as he could and then took a plane to get some pictures of the storm damage from above and cover this big story.

The road was very icy, and it was slow going from Omaha to Grand Island, where Cowan spent the night. The highway was clear at North Platte the next day, and the weather was mild, but when he reached Ogallala, the road was blocked. Cowan, along with about two thousand other travelers, holed up in the town. The few places there were to eat were packed with people, so Cowan ate very little, mostly candy bars and hamburgers.

The blizzard was exceedingly hard and hazardous to cover, since it was difficult to reach the other sides of snow-blocked roads. Having made it to Ogallala, Cowan was lucky to have Bill Ingrams take him in along with eleven other stranded travelers, who all shared a four-room house.

Since the travelers had nothing to do but wait, talk abounded—on their inconveniences, where they were headed and if more snow was coming their way. Every conversation was a bit different, but they always came back to the extent of the snow-covered roads ahead, the location of the snowplows and who might be out there in the cold, possibly freezing to death. Cowan, however, had traveled to the storm as a reporter, and he had a job to do. He continued:

> *I drove as far as I could—a short distance west of Brule, nine miles from Ogallala. A double line of vehicles, all headed west, blocked the way. Far ahead a small rotary snow plow sought to grind through a drift 50 yards long, 20 to 25 feet high. A long walk to the plow. Six pictures in 10 minutes. Back down the road highway workers put a fence across the road to hold back the eager beavers. A knot of angry travelers clustered about Highway Engineer W.L. Fisk. They demanded that he let them go through open prairie around the big drifts. Some of them had been waiting for days. They said nasty things about our State Highway Department.*[28]

Although it was understandable that the travelers were getting irritated after being stranded for so long, driving across the prairie did not prove to be a way out for some who just got stuck. If Cowan wanted to get photographs of the storm, he was going to have to take them from above.

Many of the pilots in the area were busy going on rescue missions, so no one seemed to have the time to take a reporter from the *World-Herald* up to take a look around—that is until Cowan found Frank Peters, an Ogallala rancher. Peters took Cowan up in his plane, and they flew for a couple of hours. Cowan got some photographs while Peters looked for distress signals—none were found.

The next week, Cowan was able to get a flight to Gordon from Bill Poncelow: "We made a stab at starting on the afternoon of January 11. Weather was foggy. Mist froze on the windshield and wings. After 10 miles, we couldn't see forward and turned back."[29]

The weather had cleared by the next morning, and Cowan was able to capture some remarkable pictures of the storm for the *Omaha World-Herald*. His next stop was Harrison, which was still blanketed with snow. The people there had no way out. Cowan could not get a plane out of Gordon, so he sent for help. Soon, Chris Christenson arrived in a small Cessna plane, and they were off, taking several aerial pictures of the snow-covered landscape.

The last leg of the journey took Cowan back to Omaha with the photographs and story the *World-Herald* was waiting for. He was tired from his journey and, he said, very hungry.

Although Omaha did not suffer as badly as western Nebraska did during the January 3–4 blizzard, the steadfast reporters from the *Omaha World-Herald* were working hard to get the news out to the areas that did. They traveled more than one thousand miles by ground and two thousand miles by air to cover the story.[30] Some newspapers, like the *Chadron Record*, had previously written about how lucky its area had been to miss the first two snowstorms. Chadron was not so lucky this time.

Robert Phipps in the *Omaha World-Herald*'s special edition from January 1949 reported the following interesting storm news from around the state.

According to the *Chadron Record*, a man who lived through the blizzard of '88 was adamant in proclaiming that this storm of '49 was worse than the one in '88. Bill Kohler, who had bragged about how his four-wheel-drive Jeep could take him anywhere, soon found himself stuck in the snow a couple of miles from Chadron; however, Pete Henkens, who made the same claim about his crawler tractor, proved he could get through anything. Henkens even took the hose cart to the firetruck out on a call to North Morehead.

The *Keith County News* reported that Ogallala was the end of the line for many travelers, which caused telephone usage to skyrocket. There were seventeen telephone operators on duty to handle call after call. Each operator put in a long eighteen-hour shift and managed to connect thirteen thousand calls in just one day. (A normal day would have seen them connecting around just five thousand.)

Bob Stuckman and Alice Dressler had planned to get married, but they did not plan on the blizzard stopping them. Bob's determination to make it to his own wedding in Brule pushed him to travel by car, tractor and horse. The nuptials proceeded, but there was a seven-hour delay in the service.

An enterprising soldier who found himself stranded and nearly out of money decided his best option was to buy a snow shovel and see how much scooping he could do for people. He made twenty-three dollars and got a free meal before the end of the day.

A pilot reported a peculiar rescue mission in which he flew his Piper Cub forty miles to retrieve the body of a rancher who had died two days prior.

The plane had some difficulties and banked, which gave the pilot a shock, as he found himself receiving a strange kind of embrace from the corpse.

Another pilot received an unconventional offer from a Sandhills rancher, as mentioned in the *North Platte Telegraph-Bulletin*. The rancher had evidently run out of whiskey and said he would let the aviator name his price if he would just fly over and do an air drop of two bottles.

Amos Ross had an income tax form to file, so he started walking the fourteen miles to town. It took him a day and a half, but he did not miss his filing deadline.

From the *Polk Progress*: the storm did not miss this area either. Mr. and Mrs. Will Kroger had a standpipe near their home overflow, causing five of the big elm trees in their area to be completely covered in ice.

From the *Bridgeport News-Blade*: even though the community of Dalton had a population of only four hundred, it was able to provide food and lodging for about two hundred travelers.

According to the *Lodge Pole Express*: eight people who found themselves stranded in Dalton started a game of pitch on Sunday night. They had a couple of beds that they took turns sleeping in, but they kept playing cards until Thursday morning.

From the *O'Neill Frontier*: a funeral here was postponed not once, not twice but three times due to bad weather.

From the *Lincoln Country Tribune* of North Platte: Don Reynolds made it to town, but he had to use a car, a tractor, a truck and a horse.

The *Alliance Times-Herald* informed its readers that a woman who had lost track of the days sent out word during the blizzard that she really needed a calendar.

The *Stapleton Enterprise* included the story of Fred Reckard, who lived by himself and did not have a telephone at his residence. He was not feeling well during the storm, and as his condition worsened, he thought he needed to see a doctor, so he walked the nine and a half miles into town.

From the *Sheridan County Star*: Mabel Grimes said, "It's a pretty good feeling for our town and community to have that we fought the elements together with cheerfulness, willing hands and hearts, and no one put up a squawk. We upheld that tradition—we take care of our community in good times or bad, sharing and helping with pride."[31]

Every year, when the cold, snowy weather crawls across the state of Nebraska, blizzard stories abound, but the stories about the snow and high winds from the once-in-a-generation winter storm of 1948–49 have been told and retold for many years.

A dog investigates a pickup buried by a snowbank in Custer County. Only the door of the vehicle can be seen. *History Nebraska.*

According to an article in the *Pierce County Leader* from January 20, 1949, the winds and freezing cold temperatures were the main reason the roads did not remain open after the snowplows went through. "State roads, county roads, and railroads have not had a 'breathing spell' since our first taste of winter hit this area on November 18th."[32]

It was best to stay home, but this was impossible for some. Two doctors from the Pierce area needed to reach the sick and traveled using whatever means they could find. They would start out in an automobile, use a tractor or sometimes a horse and wagon and then walk the rest of the way. Mail carriers, too, could get only so far. Help was given by many individuals who, along the way, picked up several bundles and distributed the mail to neighbors by horse or tractor or on foot.

Due to this immobility, feeding livestock became a major problem. Some of the animals should have gone to market, but they were trapped on the farm; therefore, they had to be fed and kept alive at a time when, normally, they would have been sold weeks prior. Hay was hard to find—literally. Any haystacks that had been stored near buildings were buried in snowdrifts and tough to retrieve. Haybales that had been put up in bottomlands were impossible to reach. Picked corn in windrows was nowhere in sight under the snow. These increasing feed costs cut deeply into profits, making farmers even more impatient to get through the impassable roads.

Fuel was another problem. The tank wagons that carried filling station fuel shadowed the plows as they opened the roads each day. Tank drivers would go as far out of town as they could. Customers would then have to get to the fuel tanks any way they could, often hauling empty barrels across snowy fields with wagons and teams of horses.

Telephone calls to county commissioners started early in the morning and continued throughout day. People wanted to know when their roads were going to be opened. Plow operators worked long shifts during these cold, snowy days that crippled transportation. Those who called to let people know they had a sick person at their house were put on a priority list, and the snowplows headed in their direction. Plow drivers were also keenly aware of any households that were expecting a baby and prioritized those roads as well, but in these adverse weather conditions, the newly opened roads were clear for only a few hours until the blowing snow filled them in again.

The *Leader* reported the following:

> *The county owned road opening equipment has been bogged down due to the unprecedented coating of sleet and ice that has covered the area. The crust and snow drifts will often hold the equipment on its surface for 20 or 30 feet and then with a sudden jolt break through the crust. The operators must then fight their way backwards out of the drift to solid ground before they can work forward again.*[33]

Railroads had their share of difficulties with lines that were nearly impossible to navigate. The *Leader* continued:

> *The sleet storm of a week ago crusted the rails with a heavy coating of ice that is packed hard enough to lift the wheel flanges of engines and cars right off the rails. On three separate occasions the Chicago & Northwestern snow plow engines have had to fill with water here in Pierce as they were unable to proceed to Foster, where the first water tower out of Norfolk is maintained by the railroad. The double header engines each will hold from 4,000 to 6,000 gallons of water and must be filled from a fire hydrant. On one trip from Norfolk the snow plow was derailed 11 times and due to the same handicap required a half day to reach Foster from Pierce. One railroader in Pierce said it was the first time in his 30 years' experience that*

A Union Pacific train in between Genoa and Columbus after yet another snowstorm during the winter of 1948–49. *Platte County Historical Society.*

he had ever seen a double header sent out to buck snow drifts only 12 inches deep, and to top it off "the plow didn't get through." [34]

When one takes into account the damage to trains and snow-clearing equipment along with extra hours of labor, extra feed to livestock on farms and lost business due to the storm, the cost of the blizzard of 1948–49 is impossible to assess.

Thousands of farmers and ranchers, some snowbound for several weeks and already suffering from gnawing hunger, now faced the real prospect of starvation unless something dramatic was done soon. Even worse was the prospect of tens of millions of livestock dying from exposure and starvation, which, if allowed to occur, would devastate Nebraska's billion-dollar agricultural economy.

Local citizens, volunteer firemen, policemen, private pilots and charitable organizations like the American Red Cross, not wanting to wait for the generosity of the federal government, decided to take the proverbial bull by the horns and do something about it. A few inventive local businessmen and grocery store owners, some of whom were World War II veterans, got their hands on a number of army surplus vehicles. One of these vehicles was the Weasel, which was basically a modified Jeep with tank tracks on its sides in place of wheels. The advantage of this vehicle in particular, with its light weight and traction, was its ability to travel over tall snowbanks and not fall through. This enabled it to travel to places that horses, cars and bulldozers could not reach.[35]

These enterprising businessmen loaded these Weasels up with as much dry goods and produce as they could carry and took their stores over the road to the customers. Farmers would pay for the deliveries with cash or barter with produce like fresh eggs, milk, cheese or butter.

Private pilots coordinated with radio stations or dropped leaflets to tell farmers how to use coal or wood to write in the snow or paint words on bedsheets so they could tell pilots who flew overhead exactly what they needed to drop down. Whether it was supplies, like food, gasoline, diesel or coal, or someone who needed medical attention, these brave pilots would do what they could to deliver much-needed assistance to those who needed help. But they could deliver only minuscule amounts, since private planes could carry only so much weight.

A farm shed completely covered by snow. Going anywhere by automobile or on foot was highly unlikely during the worst of the storms. *History Nebraska.*

When it came to rescuing people who needed medical attention, that required a lot of special planning in advance. Fields had to be cleared so pilots could land and take off safely with their fragile human cargo. Some planes had to be modified with skis instead of rubber tires so they could land on the snow cover a little more gently.

The heavy snow and arctic air caused plenty of hardships for humans, but it took a toll on the livestock as well. A small number of farmers attempted to recoup their cattle losses by harvesting the meat from cows that had suffocated in the field or had frozen to death in the snowy environment. Because the meat had been frozen, they thought it would not be tainted and sold it to local butcher shops and grocery stores, which were happy to have the meat, as there were widespread delays in their regular shipments.[36]

Normally, when an animal went to a slaughterhouse to be butchered, it would immediately be dissected and hung on a hook to allow it to bleed out. It would then be sprayed off with clean water to make sure no feces, stomach acids or other bodily fluids remained on the meat before it was processed. When these cows died in the field, they would often lay there for quite some time before they were butchered. The stomach acids and other fluids had time to ferment and seep into the carcasses, which caused the meat to become contaminated.[37] Inspectors soon realized this was a major problem, and health departments sent out notices to examine meat before eating it. Anything that was darker in color should be discarded in order to avoid food poisoning.

Since the first blizzard on November 18, 1948, new storms with deadly winds continued to burden the Great Plains states until even the enduring spirits of the people of Nebraska began to deteriorate. It was generally felt that recovery was entirely possible after the January 3 blizzard, but with snow that kept piling up and winds that kept blowing, people were being pushed to the limits of human endurance. Trails blew shut again and again, supplies and fuel ran low, cattle became isolated from feed and there was no end in sight. But the people would not give up easily.

An article by Max Coffey in the *Omaha World-Herald*'s special edition for the blizzard of 1949 gave a summary of the state of affairs thus far:

> *Feed supplies, inadequate for the longest winter some of the ranchers ever had known, were getting down to the last wisps of hay on some ranches. Protein feeds had run out. Cattle that had been standing stiff-legged on ice-covered snow for week upon week were emaciated and footsore, literally half-frozen and half-starved. And in many areas there was no*

telling how much human suffering was going on, how many people needed relief, how many were sick. These were secrets locked behind impenetrable barriers of snow.[38]

To understand the magnitude of the tasks that clearing roads and trying to save cattle were, Coffey provided figures on the area that was covered, including the number of people in each region and the number of cattle affected.

In Nebraska—an area of 52,346 square miles containing 521,891 people and 2,521,000 cattle. In South Dakota—an area of 40,765 square miles containing 157,000 people and 810,900 cattle. In Wyoming—an area of 45,760 square miles, containing 138,387 people and 460,000 cattle. Within these areas totaling nearly 140,000 square miles were an estimated 250,000 miles of roads, ranging from primary highways to mere wheel tracks into isolated ranches.[39]

Reality began to dawn on people: the only way to get life back to normal, save the vast multitude of human and animal lives in danger and protect Nebraska's fragile farming sector was to convince the Nebraska state legislature, along with the federal government, that immediate emergency action was needed. Despite the selfless and superhuman efforts of many brave individuals, the state needed to mobilize the Nebraska National Guard and the U.S. Army Corps of Engineers.

Frustrations grew quickly, especially among small business owners whose incomes were ravaged when the incessant snowfall and winds prevented customers from coming to their stores on a regular basis. It was not that cities and counties lacked snow moving equipment, they just did not have enough of it—certainly not enough to suffice in this most extreme of winters. Naturally, some areas felt that their particular region was being ignored by local and state authorities in favor of other areas. In a calamity such as this, workers could not be everywhere at once, and someone always felt slighted.

A growing chorus of Nebraska citizens, from farmers, ranchers, low-wage workers and business owners to state senators and journalists, felt it was time to ask for federal help. This was hard for a state that prided itself on its self-reliance and independence. It was humbling for the state to admit it needed some outside assistance. Private inquiries were made to Governor Val Peterson; many suggested he should contact President

Harry Truman, as well as the state offices of the U.S. Army Corps of Engineers. This winter had degenerated from a season of inconvenience to a life-or-death fight.

Governor Val Peterson, by this time, had declared a state of emergency in twenty-two Nebraska counties, as well as parts of seven other counties, and requested information about road conditions in different areas of Nebraska. Citizens were concerned about the disruption of supply chains in their communities. People needed fuel, doctors needed to reach patients and livestock needed to be fed. To encourage and expedite legislative operations, the community of Pierce responded to the governor's inquiry regarding their circumstances with the following telegram:

TELEGRAM

To:
Governor Val Peterson,
State House,
Lincoln, Nebraska

With one snow plow on heavy tractor and one snow plow on road maintenance, we have been able to partially give one-way traffic in south half of Pierce County until last week. After roads have been opened from three to four times we must now abandon roads and try open fields. Road maintainer is useless for this open field work. Answering emergency sick calls has taken fifty percent of our heavy snow plow time, leaving little time to devote to roads. We need assistance badly. Feed for cattle is in county but cannot be reached. Situation is fast becoming critical. We have hired local bulldozer, only one obtainable, which will help but in no way relieve emergency. Present equipment cannot open roads in time for even late spring thaw when trails opened in fields will be useless. Such period would last at least thirty days, creating a second emergency. Need four to five days rotary work for cleanup. Financial standing is very sad indeed.

Roy Bovee, County Commissioner, Third Dist.
Pierce County, Nebraska
Bill Cox, Mayor of Pierce, Nebraska[40]

Another potentially even more serious emergency was the spring thaw. It would soon make traveling across fields impossible and impede transportation worse than the snow had. It was also likely that the snowmelt would cause flooding. Roads needed to be opened, or the disastrous situation would only deteriorate.

Plows and people had been working continuously since the first blizzard on November 18 to clear the roads, but the January snow was unrelenting as it blocked newly opened roads again and again. To make matters worse, sometimes, rain fell on top of the packed snow, causing a layer of ice to form on the surface. Financial losses grew, and livestock suffered from the feed shortage. Nebraskans could potentially lose hundreds of millions of dollars.

Everyone hoped and prayed for a turn in the weather, but mild weather seemed unlikely in January. Governor Val Peterson heard requests from mayors and city leaders pleading for assistance. With supply chains slowed or not running at all, it looked like the coming weeks would see millions of cattle, sheep and pigs starving to death due to a lack of hay and grain before the spring thaw. Estimates were that cattle losses could run as high as 40 percent, and with calves being born soon, that number was set to rise.[41]

To avoid these vast losses of livestock and more human suffering, the governor knew he had to act quickly. He met with members of the Nebraska legislature and the Department of Roads to formulate a plan, asking the U.S. Army Corps of Engineers and the Fifth Army for the use of any heavy equipment along with the manpower needed to run them. He requested the budget committee to allocate an emergency fund of over $500,000 in emergency aid to communities hit the hardest, provided snow-clearing equipment could be acquired and put to use. The money was appropriated.[42]

Communities were grateful when state aid finally came through, along with more road-clearing equipment and the help of the Fifth Army. A complete plan of action was agreed on, and orders were given to open roads, making no farmhouse any farther than two miles away from an accessible road; however, with ice capping the top of the snow, even twenty-ton bulldozers made little headway when working against the resistant ice-covered drifts.

The equipment plowed and pushed snow to the side, where it could have easily taken out fences or telephone poles had it not been for the assistance of local guides who were familiar with the land. It was especially important to have help while crossing bridges. With the massive amounts of ice on the bridge rails, bulldozers could have torn into them without realizing it. Farmers and other citizens in the community also assisted with snowplow crews, and they opened their homes to those who had traveled across the state to help, warming them and providing hot meals and coffee. The plan was to open roads to within one mile of each farmhouse after the two-mile

Above: Governor Val Peterson (*center*) in a military briefing. Nebraska urgently needed snow moving equipment along with manpower and federal aid. *History Nebraska*.

Opposite: Governor Peterson on an airplane tour over Nebraska. After seeing the extreme conditions from the air, he asked President Truman for help. *History Nebraska*.

goal was reached. They needed help from the government to press on and free trails on farms and ranches to get animals to feed sources.

President Truman, however, was not as quick to provide federal aid to the state as the governor would have liked. In Nebraska, there was not enough funding to accomplish this task on the scale that was needed. Several representatives from Nebraska—and some from neighboring states—failed to pry off the red tape and get an audience with the president to impress on him just how dire the situation was. Although Truman did promise road-clearing equipment, he did not want to provide any federal funding.[43]

Penetrating these layers of bureaucracy took time, and time was one thing Nebraskans did not have. Governor Peterson was able to send Agricultural Director Rufus Howard to impress on President Truman the urgent need for funding, as millions of livestock would perish if something was not done immediately. In Congress, however, a House subcommittee

wanted to check into weather records to see if this winter was any more severe than prior winters. Truman initially ignored requests that the project be turned over to Major General Lewis Pick and instead appointed Major General Philip Fleming of the Federal Works Administration to coordinate federal relief efforts.[44]

General Fleming seemed unconcerned with the urgency of the request and headed to Miami, Florida, for a conference of the American

Federation of Labor. Fleming was photographed wearing short sleeves, enjoying the warm Florida weather.[45] It was not until the end of January, after the report from Fleming was finally given to the president, that the president felt pressured enough to act. The secretary of defense was ordered to use whatever money and resources were necessary to alleviate this state of emergency. Federal relief was now headed toward Nebraska, and Operation Snowbound was born.

4

OPERATION SNOWBOUND

Major General Lewis A. Pick of the U.S. Army Corps of Engineers, Missouri Division, was in charge. He had the privilege of commanding this daunting operation and taking responsibility for lining up all the men and equipment that would be needed. This was by no means Pick's first rodeo. Years earlier, he had been in charge of building the Ledo Road in between China and India, which got him noticed as an outstanding engineering officer during World War II. He was also experienced in building Missouri River dams in the intervening years.

Even before federal help arrived, Governor Val Peterson coordinated a headquarters office for Operation Snowbound in the basement of the capitol in Lincoln. The national guard, under the command of Guy Denninger, directed the Nebraska office, while the federal office, when it was established a week later under the command of General Pick, was located in Omaha.[46]

The Lincoln location worked as the liaison office for local, state and federal advisors, who forwarded hour-by-hour updates, along with news of what equipment was working where, what supplies were needed and what highways had been cleared. The grand-scale devastation of Nebraska's countryside and the critical need for help still may not have been clear to army and air force officers until they were taken on an aerial tour of the encased, frozen landscape. It was hard to believe that anyone could survive such widespread misery.

With federal relief on its way, the army and the Nebraska National Guard brought in all the vehicles they had available: road maintainers, bulldozers, dump trucks and Weasels. Much credit must be given to those who lived in the areas with impassable roads, as they knew the land and were able to direct military personnel through the stricken areas, letting them know the location of bridges, roads and farmhouses that were cut off by the snow.

Operation Snowbound was described as a last resort born of necessity. When General Pick was finally given the go-ahead for Operation Snowbound, he was expecting the job and was well prepared. He had already been planning a campaign to organize his forces into immediate action. Even before word officially came to him that he would be responsible for leading the operation, he sent reconnaissance teams to search for and gather information.

District engineers were ready and put into place. Pick knew how to divide the massive territory and set up subdivisions and headquarter towns for each division, utilizing as much local help as he could get. According to Max Coffey in a special edition of the *Omaha World-Herald*, Pick was quoted as saying, "Operation Snowbound is a job everybody's got to help out on."[47]

Community members were tired of this battle against the elements, and they were more than happy to offer their hands to work for a coordinated agency that would direct them. Operation Snowbound and General Pick, as a central authority, found local people and organizations that were willing to help as well, such as newspapers, the Soil Conservation Service, independent pilots, farmers, veterinarians, flying organizations, the Bureau of Reclamation, labor unions, medical societies, the national guard and the American Red Cross.

To get operations underway and progressing quickly, General Pick made telephone calls to private contractors all over the state. He requested the use of their equipment along with operators who knew how to run bulldozers and snowplows. When the machines arrived, he used his chain of command to dispatch them to subareas and then on to local commanders.

Coffey reported: "At his first press conference, the day the big job began, General Pick predicted that Operation Snowbound 'probably will wind up as the next biggest bulldozer operation after the Ledo Road….There it was the rain, heat, and mud; here it is snow, ice, and cold.'"[48] It is important to mention that General Pick did come to believe that Operation Snowbound was a bigger bulldozer operation than the one he put together during the construction of the Ledo Road that connected India and China.

Military council in the Custer County Courthouse in Broken Bow. The two men in uniform are Captain G.A. Schrader (*left*) and Major C.E. Cross (*right*). *History Nebraska.*

By February 3, Coffey reported that "673 bulldozers, 123 snowplows and patrols, and 116 Army Weasels were either at work in the snowbound area or on their way in."[49] Bulldozers were appearing from places like Denver, Kansas City, Billings, Saint Paul and every town in between that had any snow moving equipment to spare.

In conjunction with Operation Snowbound was Operation Haylift, which was a program designed to literally drop haybales as close to livestock as possible from C-47 and C-82 planes. Riding along in the cockpit with air force personnel were local farmers or ranchers who were familiar with the area and could direct the plane to the farms in need of assistance, so they could drop their cargo near the starving cattle. Five to seven additional civilian "kickers" were also brought along on these flights. These were people who strapped themselves to the bulkheads of the planes and were in charge of kicking the hay out of the open cargo doors when they were above the herds.[50]

When the spotter indicated the right place for the drop, the pilot would hit a buzzer to let the kickers know it was time to push the hay out of the cargo bay. These flights were a bit dangerous, but the pilots and civilians alike enjoyed the adventure of the low-level flights and the idea that they were doing something to make a difference.

Small helicopters like this, with their maneuverability and ability to fly low, played an important role in Operation Snowbound. *History Nebraska.*

Operation Haylift seemed like a good idea in theory, but it may not have worked as well as predicted. Governor Peterson thought it was more of a publicity stunt, as the cattle could not maneuver through the ice-covered and drifted fields to reach the hay that may have fallen within one hundred yards of them. The low-flying planes also startled herds and caused them to run from the life-saving hay being dropped. It did, however, provide a temporary way to reach some cattle and keep them fed for a while until ground crews could deliver more hay and feed, sometimes pulled by hand on a toboggan, to the starving animals.[51]

The most effective path to relief was, of course, ground-based transportation. Bulldozers and snowplows did the heavy lifting of pushing snow off the roads to make way for semitrucks, pickups and cars that were transporting people and cargo to not just reach citizens in need but also to open regular supply lines, returning some sense of normality to the winter-weary people of Nebraska.

People wanted to be able to drive to work and get there on time. Country children were eager to be able to walk or ride to school to see their classmates and teachers again. Everyone looked forward to the return of social functions, such as church services, ballroom dances or just regular visits with friends and family. Places like King's Ballroom in Norfolk, which normally drew crowds from neighboring cities to listen to performers like Guy Lombardo and Lawrence Welk, were ready to welcome the people back.

This leads us to the ugly truth about why the winter of 1948–49 was so devastating to the Great Plains, including Nebraska: the primitive state of rural roads and motor vehicles slowed progress. To start, concrete highways and automobiles as we know them today had only existed for roughly twenty-five to thirty years. Although the first car was built in Germany in 1885, it was nothing more than a toy for the rich and daredevils until the Ford Model T was invented in 1908. This was the first mass-produced, reliable and, most importantly, affordable automobile for the masses.

Before the Model T, car owners had to literally employ their own mechanic or know how to fix and maintain the automobile on their own. Although car technology had advanced greatly by 1948, people were still handicapped by the fact that their engines were powered by carburetors, which had to squirt just the right mixture of air and gasoline vapor into the engine for the car to run.[52] This was problematic even in perfect weather conditions, but during the frigid months of a winter, engines ran poorly—or worse, they did not start at all.

Unless a person was lucky enough to get their hands on an army surplus vehicle, few vehicles made by manufacturers had four-wheel drive. Since cars were rear-wheel drive at the time, it was difficult to impossible to drive

This photograph shows King's Ballroom in Norfolk. Northeast Nebraska bore much of the brunt of the winter of 1948–49. *Elkhorn Valley Museum.*

over an ice- or snow-crusted road, sending many unlucky motorists into a ditch, tree or other vehicle during treacherous winter driving conditions.

Adding to this misery was the fact that most vehicles in America were over ten or fifteen years old. During the Great Depression of the 1930s, most Americans could not afford to buy a new vehicle. Following that, during the United States' involvement in World War II, car manufacturers stopped making new models altogether so they could concentrate on making military vehicles, such as Jeeps, troop trucks, tanks and aircraft. In addition to this, there was gas rationing during the war, which made the demand for new vehicles minuscule.

The automobiles themselves, however, were only half of the problem. Although most of the cities and towns in Nebraska at the time had paved or brick streets, the state's country roads were not in good shape. The roads on the outskirts of towns and those that led into the country, usually made of gravel or dirt, made up about 95 percent of the one hundred thousand miles of roads in Nebraska.[53]

New road construction in the United States during the Great Depression and on into World War II had mostly stopped. Some funding existed in the 1940s for repairs and maintenance, but it never seemed to be anything more than the bare minimum. Road crews did what they could to preserve existing bridges and highways, but they did only enough to get by without actually improving the conditions. They were just trying to avoid a state of complete disrepair.

General Lewis Pick, having previously been in charge of work on the immense Missouri River dams, was well aware of the challenges facing him with the blocked roads in Nebraska and was prepared to enlist the services of any civilians who were willing to work through his chain of command. When he had been in charge of work on the dams, he had accomplished the construction of engineering marvels that would regulate the snowmelt from Montana and through the Dakotas along the Missouri River. Now, he would employ the same proactive techniques that succeeded in building the massive man-made dams.[54]

Pick's organizational skills required each person to know their part. He and his men would use the best piece of equipment for each area, choosing between a bulldozer or a maintainer to be the most efficient for the task. He was also careful in selecting exactly the right man for each job, believing the key to success with Operation Snowbound would be to pair up army personal with civilians, creating a good relationship between the miliary and the locals who volunteered to help.

A car travels along a road just outside of Pierce. Older vehicles and poor road conditions made going anywhere even more difficult. *Elkhorn Valley Museum.*

Machines were maintained by hand-picked staff, and Pick was dedicated to brainstorming with forward-thinkers to figure out ahead of time which parts would likely need to be replaced or repaired so he could order the right spare parts in advance. Anything he thought would eventually break down would not have to wait for repairs, and there would be no slowing down in the completion of his assignment.

As a World War II veteran, General Pick had experience with working with local officials and keeping up with regular progress reports. During the war, he knew that reporting the number of miles recaptured from the Germans and Japanese by the Allies in Europe or Pacific Islands had boosted the morale of American citizens back home who were eager to hear any good news. With Operation Snowbound, he wanted to keep morale high by making sure that local officials were informed with daily reports on how many miles of roads were cleared each day.[55]

Pick chose to start with the worst counties first, using many army Weasels to reach places where bulldozers and other heavy equipment could not get through. The Weasel, according to some, was the key to recovery in Nebraska. It had a Jeep-like body and used tank tracks instead of rubber tires. It could have an open cab or an enclosed canopy, yet the tank tracks provided the needed traction to cross the icy terrain, and the unit was lightweight enough to be able to travel across the high snowdrifts without falling through.[56]

Although the Weasels were unable to push snow, they were indispensable in reaching people in snow-locked areas and getting them much-needed supplies. They were also most helpful in getting to those in need of medical care, like women who were in labor or folks who required an immediate surgery or hospitalization for an appendectomy or a broken leg that needed to be set in a cast.

The provisions given to families by the Red Cross included items such as sugar, flour, salt, butter, oatmeal, lard, coffee, bacon, beans and soap.[57] These items and many more were brought to farmhouses on Weasels led by local guides familiar with the area, similar to those who helped with Operation Haylift. Although Weasels were initially designed by the Allied forces to navigate the winter driving conditions in Norway if and when they decided to attack the Nazi-occupied region, the army found Weasels were most useful as a lightweight vehicle that could be airlifted into regions, and it was durable enough to hold up to a parachute drop. They were amphibious and could easily travel over muddy, soft ground that Jeeps could not reach.[58]

Army Weasels had the best of both worlds: they had tank tracks to give them traction but were light enough to drive over snowbanks. *History Nebraska.*

Although it could transverse muddy, sandy and rocky terrains, the Weasel was specifically designed to travel through snow-covered areas and could pull a sled loaded with cargo.[59] This being the case, it came as no surprise that the Weasel was the vehicle of choice for the army's rescue and supply operations during Operation Snowbound in the frozen fields of Nebraska, where no other machine could go.

For larger deliveries, Weasels brought fresh cow's milk to dairy processing facilities and cut meat to butchers. It took patients to hospitals and doctors to house calls out in the country. They also helped with transporting the mail to areas where the postal service was not able to get through. While the vehicle was made for the Allied forces in World War II, the Weasel was an indispensable vehicle to many communities affected by the deadly winter storms during Operation Snowbound.

As mentioned in the *Pierce County Leader* article from January 1949 "Weasels Make Mercy Mission," Lieutenant John D. Bievines led a crew of five army men to the Pierce area. They were on duty day and night to keep the two Weasels they had at their disposal running. "Many of their 'missions' have been in answer to calls of Dr. J.H. Calvert and Dr. W.I. Devers....The two Weasels have traveled over a thousand miles since they arrived here two weeks ago."[60]

Army Weasels were built as hybrid vehicles with a Jeep chassis and tank tracks. Weasels brought supplies to many snowbound people. *History Nebraska.*

The lightweight machines did not provide much protection from the bitter cold, but the men who drove bulldozers had even worse hardships, as they had no cab or windshield to block the brutal winter conditions. These drivers were often on the road for ten hours at a time, which was bad enough during the day, but it was even worse at night, when temperatures would plummet as low as twenty degrees below zero. With snow and ice flying into their faces part of the time, it is a wonder that any of these so called catskinners managed to survive.

Bulldozer and snowplow crews soon discovered that if they pushed the snow into sloped, diagonal banks instead of tall vertical piles, the drifting would be somewhat reduced. They also learned that because of the northerly prevailing winds, the roads going east and west tended to get blocked by drifting snow more frequently than the north–south roads, so plowing priority had to be allocated to the east–west ones.[61]

Another myth that was quickly shattered was the belief that if an area was lucky enough to get a day or two of above-freezing temperatures, the inch or two of crust melt on the snow's surface would prevent any further drifting. With the stubborn winds that blew continuously during the winter of 1948–49, once the temperature dropped below freezing again, the icy crust would quickly erode into a granular, powdery form, restarting the blowing and drifting of snow.[62]

With the hundreds of experienced men driving snowplows and bulldozers for long working days and freeing the snow drifted roads and highways in Nebraska, progress was underway. After Nebraskans spent weeks of being snowbound, with transportation hindered due to impassable roads, much-needed supplies were able to go where they needed to go. People began traveling to work and visiting neighbors and family members for enjoyment. Things were beginning to look a bit brighter.

However, this horrendous winter in Nebraska produced a massive number of deaths in the livestock market. The fear of a meat shortage due to possibly losing even more cattle to the persistent, freezing conditions led to sky-high prices in an uncertain market. With Operation Snowbound in full force and the roads finally cleared to feedlots and pastures, cattlemen loaded as many cows as they could cram into trailers for immediate sale at livestock markets.

At the time, no one knew if the winter was over or if Nebraska was in for an even longer and more severe season of ice and snow. Why take a chance on losing even more cattle to the elements? With a sudden logjam, everyone had cattle for sale, which led to a sharp drop in prices and, after having a shortage for many weeks, an oversupply of meat.[63] These dramatic price swings were great for savvy meat brokers or consumers who timed their meat purchases right, but they were not so great for those who were unlucky enough to buy at the wrong time.

The title from the following article in the February 10, 1949 *Pierce County Leader* highlights the advancement of Operation Snowbound:

Road Opening Progresses Slowly as Snow Drifts

The gigantic job of opening the roads in this area is still steadily marching forward but the job is far from completed. Snow blows back into the cleared roads at every wind as the fences and trees are clogged full and no longer holds the drifting snow. Attempts to open hay lands in the bottom area have been very slow with the heavy type equipment due to the excessive weight of the "cats" which run from 18 to 26 tons. There is little or no frost under the snow and the "cats" tend to bog down.[64]

Miles of roads continued to be opened and then blocked again due to the wind carrying loose snow across previously cleared areas. It was soon discovered that rotary plows were more useful than straight plows in reopening snow-covered roads, as they could toss the snow up and out of the way instead of just pushing it to the side.

Everyone just wanted to help as many people as they could as quickly as possible. The system created in the northeastern part of the state was to run bulldozers as much as possible, opening up roads and then returning to free snow from lanes, pastures and hay fields. Airplanes and Weasels responded to calls for help from the sick or those in desperate need of supplies.

According to the same February 10, 1949 *Leader* article: "The 'Weasels' stationed here in Pierce have been the work horses of emergencies. They have hauled medicine, groceries, hay, coal and many other items that were desperately needed and transported doctors to their patients."[65]

Although progress was apparent, it was not yet possible to begin thinking about an end date for Operation Snowbound. There was a never-ending number of roads that needed to be opened, people who needed medicine and fuel and livestock that needed hay.

Honoring his promise to keep people informed of his progress regarding Operation Snowbound, General Pick held news conferences to present the most recent developments. Max Coffey recounted them as follows:

> *February 1 (third day after Operation Snowbound had been authorized): 206 miles of road cleared, 1,686 snowbound persons liberated.*
> *February 2: 1,097 miles of road opened, 4,856 persons liberated, 150,000 cattle given access to feed.*
> *February 3: 3,551 miles of road opened, 7,846 persons given outlets from their snowbound homes, 195,890 cattle provided with access to feed.*
> *February 4: 9,180 miles of road opened, 25,131 persons freed from isolation, 550,740 cattle given access to feed.*[66]

This progress did not mean that the operation would be coming to an end anytime soon. There was more snow falling and high winds that freed whirlwinds of flurries from the hard, icy snowbanks and reclosed roads numerous times.[67] Pick was watchful of these ground blizzards, because he knew they had the potential to cut off snowplows and bulldozers from refueling centers or places designated for repairs.

To counteract this continual undoing of work, Pick outlined an additional strategy that was called "a disaster plan over the disaster plan."[68] This strategy incorporated sending out surveyors to monitor conditions and figure out if blowing snow was going to shut down roads and possibly block snow-

Ground blizzards clogged roads nearly as quickly as they were opened. Crews were often sent out to prevent equipment from being cut off. *Gerald Hixson.*

clearing equipment from being able to return. Once potentially dangerous drifting was reported, more equipment would be directed to move in at once and prevent snowplows and bulldozers from being cut off.

Many local and military pilots with small planes were recruited to help with this surveying job. Their missions were twofold: they could report road conditions while completing other objectives, like reaching the sick, taking supplies to those in need or looking for new distress signals arranged in the snow.

Newspaper advertisements, radio broadcasts, word of mouth communications and even leaflets dropped by airplanes informed people on how to signal a plane that was passing overhead for help. They could lay out clothing or material to form words in the snow or use lumber to write a message large enough for the planes to see. Some people used old quilts or even spelled out words with chunks of coal. Even though most people must have been running low on supplies or were in need of something, many of the farms used what they could to write out a message indicating that all was well at their location, giving a higher priority to the relief of others.

Communications were a key ingredient of General Pick's action plan. He found the army's radio network to be invaluable, and he supplemented it with the use of mobile equipment in planes and automobiles, along with temporary communications stations set up in various field headquarters and blizzard areas. This provided fast and instant connections to all areas as needed.

Being able to make contact with other areas and dispatch equipment as needed in a timely fashion was of the utmost importance, especially in the remote areas of Nebraska where other means of communication had been disconnected due to the wintery weather. Everyone did their best to be alert to changes in road conditions as quickly as they came up.

The cooperation of the highway departments and the railroads was necessary to Operation Snowbound, because the main highways and the rails were the primary means of transporting vital supplies like food, fuel and hay. Although airplanes could deliver some supplies to individuals, they could carry only relatively small amounts, and they were not as economical as the highways and trains, which could transport large shipments.

By February 11, with federal help, ten of the counties in Nebraska that had been in the subarea reporting to the McCook headquarters were no longer considered parts of the disaster zone. Before long, another group of counties in central Nebraska was removed from the disaster classification.

A demobilization plan was in place as well. Always keeping lines of communication open between divisions and reporting to the governor before finalizing any plans, General Pick listened to officers when they announced that they believed the rest of the work could be completed by local agencies. Pick made his decision for the army to move out accordingly and contacted the governor along with the Federal Works Agency for approval. Pick would not give any orders without the consent and agreement of both.

As Operation Snowbound made progress through the state of Nebraska, cost estimates from this winter seemed to exceed any earlier predictions. According to Coffey:

> *Bookkeeping failed to keep pace with bulldozers. No accurate estimates of the total expense are available. It will run into several millions of dollars. Nebraska State Engineer Fred Klietsch in mid-February estimated that the Nebraska Highway Department would spend one million dollars for snow removal from state highways and will have to spend another million dollars to repair winter-damaged highways.* [69]

Although the disastrous storms of the winter of 1948–49 caused millions of dollars in damage, it would have cost the state millions more had it not been for the coordinated efforts of Operation Snowbound.

Operation Snowbound, led by General Lewis A. Pick, was faced with many challenges due to Nebraska's severe winter road conditions. *Elkhorn Valley Museum.*

There were heavy losses in the cattle industry, and the cows that did survive were thin and haggard. Ranchers had to remove the dead cattle that had lain in the fields during blizzard after blizzard. According to Coffey: "On February 14th the United States Department of Agriculture estimated that blizzards had killed over 81,000 cattle and 97,000 sheep in Nebraska, South Dakota, Wyoming, and Colorado."[70]

The cost of cattle dying from the horrendous conditions was only part of the losses suffered by farmers and ranchers. Stock cows generally would have gotten their nourishment from grazing in cornfields or pastures, but that did not happen this winter, and they would soon be calving. This could potentially lead to weak calves born from malnourished cows that would die from not being able to suckle, getting stuck in the mud or a variety of other reasons. Cattlemen also had to pay for the extra feed needed to keep the animals alive and build their strength back up, feed that normally would have been foraged by the cows themselves.

Similar to his command during the building of the Ledo Road, in Operation Snowbound, General Pick, along with many soldiers, came away with valuable experience. The army learned how to best deploy and run a military operation of heavy snow-moving equipment during blizzards and in subzero temperatures with high winds. They also gathered useful organizational skills regarding how to unify civilian and military personnel to accomplish a massive undertaking such as this, and they recognized ways to be flexible when strategies to repair and maintain road equipment during adverse weather conditions did not go as planned.

After twenty-three days of leading Operation Snowbound, General Pick announced his accomplishments:

> *Miles of road opened (including many re-blocked and re-opened): 87,073.*
> *Persons liberated from snowbound homes: 152,196.*
> *Sick persons taken out to receive medical care and hospitalization: 35.*
> *Livestock given access to feed: 3,598,638.*[71]

Without even considering the many local and county groups and individuals that helped, thousands of workers, many of them civilians and contractors, were involved in Operation Snowbound. Coffey continued: "At the height of operations, some 1,400 bulldozers were in operation, more than 100 motor graders, and nearly 200 Army Weasels. In Nebraska alone, 892 dozers, 53 motor graders, and 131 Weasels were employed."[72]

The first storm started in western Nebraska on November 18 and reached Omaha on November 19. The special Operation Snowbound edition of the *Omaha World-Herald* from February 1949 listed a summary of the great storms of 1948–49:

November 19: *First storm.*

December 29: *Second storm, worst in Northeast Nebraska.*

January 2–3: *The blizzard.*

January 4: *State of emergency at North Platte.*

January 11: *State of emergency declared at Gordon; Mayor L.E. Morgan addresses plea to Gov. Val Peterson to step up road clearing operations.*

January 12: *Warning sounded that cattle in dire need of feed; can't be reached because of snow-blocked fields. Governor Peterson describes storm as "the worst we ever had—almost as quickly as roads are cleared they blow shut."*

January 13: *Tenth Air Force sends in domestic emergency team. Crews opening ice-packed roads resort to dynamite.*

January 17: *Bad re-drifting occurs on Panhandle roads. Rail service blocked.*

January 18: *Re-drifting continues, area expanded.*

January 19: *Roads generally impassable west of Grand Island and north of Holdrege; snow is packed in cuts so there is no place to push it.*

January 21: *Governor Peterson meets with Legislature to discuss action; storm cost to Highway Department is 200 thousand dollars weekly.*

January 22: *Re-drifting continues. Governor Peterson appeals for additional snow removal equipment from counties outside storm, from private firms, and from the Army.*

January 23: *Snowplow crews lose most gains in new, tough winds.*

January 24: *Fresh storm hits eastern Nebraska.*

January 24: *President Truman allocates 300 thousand dollars for Missouri Basin storm relief. Governor Peterson phones President Truman, asks that Maj. Gen. Lewis A. Pick be placed in charge of emergency operations.*

January 26: *Legislature makes half-million-dollar emergency appropriation for storm.*

January 26: *President Truman appoints Maj. Gen. Philip B. Fleming, Federal Works Administrator, to handle storm relief program. General Fleming apportions 35 thousand dollars to Nebraska—cost of one day's operation of the State Highway Department.*

January 27: *General Fleming goes to sun-warmed Miami to make a speech. Nebraska allocated an additional 65 thousand dollars.*
January 28: *Maj. Gen. Lewis A. Pick named Fifth Army deputy commander to direct storm relief operations. Operation Snowbound begins.*[73]

Ralph Smith, a reporter with the *Omaha World-Herald*, accompanied several top officials, including Assistant Secretary of the Army Gordon Gray; three-star Lieutenant General Raymond A. Wheeler, chief of army engineers; Major General John P. Lucas of Chicago, deputy commander of the Fifth Army; and George H. Field of Washington's Federal Works Agency on a reconnaissance aerial tour over the blizzard-stricken areas of Nebraska on January 31.

With very little chance to survey the storm from the ground, the group was anxious to fly above the snow barrier to get a firsthand, comprehensive look at the storm damage and become better informed about the plight facing many isolated, snowbound Nebraskans. He said that what they saw was difficult to believe and offered a new perspective on the severity of the blizzards. He described the landscape as one-dimensional and under complete paralysis.

Three men are pictured by a vehicle on a road that had recently been cleared near Carroll. *Elkhorn Valley Museum.*

The day of their departure was one that seemed routine, part of each person's job. The group first met with Governor Peterson in Lincoln before embarking on their flight. Smith described their route as traveling "north through Bartlett and O'Neill to Spencer, west to Valentine, then a dogleg back to Ainsworth and a straight shot across the Sand Hills to Omaha."[74]

The Lincoln area did not appear to be much worse off than it would have been during any other winter. The blacktop highway could easily be seen as a dark strip. Graded sideroads were clearly visible, and it was relatively easy to make out farmsteads, with lanes connecting houses to the main roads. As the plane moved north, more roads became invisible, and what the men saw across most of the state was a sweeping expanse of white that stretched ominously below them.

As the day progressed, the mood of those on board the aircraft became more dispirited as they finally got to take a look at what lay past the impenetrable snow barrier. They dropped their lighthearted opinions of this snowy situation and took on a dismal view of what they soon recognized as a major crisis as their view grew more bleak with each region that was assessed from above. When they passed over the Platte River, the only noticeable guides to the river were the trees that lined its banks; otherwise, the snow had completely buried land and water alike.

The men were dismayed by the sheer amount of snow that had fallen throughout the state, but it was what Smith described as "man's effort and struggle to escape it" that was so distressing.[75] With most roads impassable, patterns of farm life could be seen from above, with trails in the snow that no longer followed the roads. Instead, people had left outlines of pathways across fields and ones that followed the tops of ridges, where the wind was the worst. The men in the airplane did not observe wheel tracks; the trails that could be seen were footpaths that led to barns, main roads, neighboring houses and country schools.

Smith reported that the flight made him feel as though he were a swimmer wading deeper and deeper into the water. The view from above was something similar to looking down on breaking waves in the ocean that had frozen in time. Telephone poles could be seen, but some were buried nearly to their tops. It was as though the group was flying over something similar to what had been seen in Admiral Byrd's documentary of his Antarctic expedition. Smith continued his report:

> *In the Spalding area township roads were blocked. In the Bartlett vicinity snow was drifted halfway up the lower sashes of farm houses. Highway*

An aerial photograph of a farm in Greeley County. The tracks leading up to the snowdrifts illustrate the family's predicament during this winter. *History Nebraska.*

281 narrowed down to one-way traffic in spots. Then snow blocks began to shut it off. At first they were relatively short. In the cleared sections traffic shuttled back and forth. Then long miles of the north–south lifeline were drifted shut.[76]

They saw the highways that had previously been cleared become lost to the blowing snow. O'Neill looked almost snug with its blanket of snow, but the men did not lose perspective and think all was well in this area, as other planes could be seen airlifting supplies to snowbound residents and providing mercy missions to those in need.

The group then turned north and headed to Spencer, Nebraska, where the storm damage was not as bad and the wind-swept areas actually showed brown earth underneath. They continued west along the Nebraska–South Dakota border to Valentine, where the cattle were scattered along sunny slopes, as opposed to huddled in groups around haystacks as the men had seen earlier.

In Valentine, the plane turned to the southeast and headed to Ainsworth. Smith described the view in this area as follows:

> *This was snow unlike that ever seen before by any one aboard. This was no soft blanket of new snow. It didn't blur and soften the sharp angles of the earth and buildings below. It didn't look like snow. It had an icy glint in the afternoon sun. It had been hammered and pounded by wind until it looked like a glacier. It has been sculptured by the wind into fantastic shapes and sharp jagged edges.*[77]

Farms were like isolated islands of humanity in a frozen world of accumulated ice and snow. Footpaths could be seen connecting buildings, wider paths to those accessed more frequently, such as barns where milk cows were housed and narrower paths to those buildings used less frequently. Sled tracks could be seen to haystacks, with nothing more than mounds of white to indicate fence lines. Any hay that had not been put away still lay in windrows, completely inaccessible and covered by the ice.

In this area, the roads did not have many clear, wind-swept spots, just a solid ice-packed barricade. The only way roads could even be spotted was by the embroidery-like outline made by the fence posts that traced a boundary on either side. There was not so much as a depression to point out the course of roads in some areas.

The talk in the plane was about the absence of the sight of any roads as they continued their tour, crossing the Sandhills area. The men silently watched and waited for some indication of a partially cleared highway, as had happened in the more northern part of their journey, but nothing materialized. All they saw on this leg of the trip was a wilderness of snow and ice.

As the day proceeded and twilight moved in, the men desperately looked for any signs of life in the Sandhills area. Even with field glasses, Smith indicated that the landscape below them on the last leg of their trip was completely snow-covered. Rationalizing that many ranchers burned oil for heat, perhaps that was the reason they did not see any smoke from chimneys.

For the last thirty-five minutes of their flight, the group grew quiet as they saw absolutely nothing to indicate any life at all existed below them. There was no smoke and no roads that could be seen, only the occasional patterns of farms—but without any signs of life. They wanted to believe that because telephone lines were still connected, the people in this remote area would check in on each other. After all, the airlift crews were still operating. It looked like the catastrophe had wiped out all life, but that didn't mean it was true.

One county in particular, Holt County, with O'Neill as its county seat, was one of the worst hit areas in Nebraska, receiving seventy inches of snow and not getting missed by a single blizzard since the first storm in November. With the county's large size and sparse and scattered population, it had the worst of both worlds. People had farther to go to rescue others, making relief efforts all the more daunting.

They also had one of the highest percentages of cattle loss in the state. According to Paul Williams in an article from the *Omaha World-Herald*, "They had probably the largest number of distressed families of any county in the disaster area—more than 350 'miniature airlift' missions had to be flown during the worst month to take emergency supplies to isolated families. They have one of the toughest road problems in Nebraska—more than 3,700 total miles of roads of all kinds."[78]

Like many Nebraskans, though, Holt Country residents proved to be enduring, resourceful and steadfast people who were kind to their neighbors and those in need. After the first blizzard, recovery from the twenty inches of snow that fell on November 19 was difficult but not impossible. With state and county road-clearing equipment, along with the help of many farmers, the county was able to open its roads and highways in two to three weeks. Neighbors looked in on each other, and those who were able to get to town for supplies brought back what was needed for others who lived nearby.

This first storm was bad, with a lot of heavy snow, but it was nothing they had not faced before. Then came the next blizzard at Christmastime—and the next starting on January 2. Pretty much every mile of road in Holt County was closed, severing ties between towns and farms. The O'Neill Airport, which was only a mile and half from town, was completely inaccessible, with at least three feet of snow and ice covering the runway. Even the railroads could not get through.

With the help of the American Legion Auxiliary, Holt County set up a basement relief headquarters to answer telephone calls and keep lines of communication open to inform people and find out who was in desperate need of cattle feed, food, fuel or medical attention. To direct where emergency supplies were needed in Holt County, Neil Dawes, a county extension agent, agreed to serve as a contact person. His job was to let those working in the Lincoln office know what was being done in his area and where help and supplies were needed.[79] Other counties followed suit and coordinated their efforts to work the same way.

Each passing week became tougher for those in Holt County. Snowstorms continued along with ground blizzards that swept across the roads, blocking them off almost as soon as they were opened. The icy, snow-packed drifts were so hard to cut through that maintainers were unable to operate without breaking down. Williams reported the following: "An Air Force snowplow from Kearney worked one entire night to get to the airport. A few days later, that plow tore out its transmission bucking drifts on a county road. A state rotary plow broke a crankshaft. An Army Weasel arrived in town, broke down the next day."[80]

County officials also organized plans for local aircraft to drop leaflets, giving stranded farmers instructions on what words to paint on bedsheets or blankets or how to create messages with whatever available material they had, be it wood, junk or spare coal nuggets, to signal to pilots. Pilots would return in a day or two to the same farms where the leaflets were dropped, read what their specific needs were and return a third time to deliver whatever supplies were needed.[81]

On January 25, Governor Peterson promised Holt County an allotment of twenty bulldozers, but bulldozers, it seemed, were in short supply, and only three arrived. The Red Cross had a distress center set up at the courthouse and arranged a meeting with whoever could make it from the county board to see what could be done to locate more resources. The board decided it would have to buy one bulldozer, and board members were able to contract the use of two more from local farmers.

Next on the board's agenda was to rent airplanes and purchase food and fuel to reach people in the blizzard-stricken area. Three pilots, Cliff Adkins, Lewis Coker and Harold Ellis, were assigned to do a house-by-house inspection of the entire 2,400 square miles of Holt County.[82] They dropped leaflets to each of these households, with instructions on how to send a message to the planes, which would then come back and make deliveries of medicine, food, fuel or whatever was needed.

Williams reported: "Two Omaha pilots—Cliff Sefton and M.B. Lorimor— came to help out. Several pilots from Yankton, S.D., flew in for brief periods of mercy flying. Airport Manager Gordon Harper and volunteer helpers worked long hours fueling, loading and dispatching the craft."[83]

The multiple blizzards that buried Nebraska this winter presented a cause-and-effect cycle that showed the overwhelming willingness of people from all over to volunteer to help in any way that they could. A pilot from Ewing named Carl Hubel used his plane to carry bulldozer parts to repair centers. His plane was damaged on his mercy missions, but people were so grateful for his efforts that they raised enough money, around $3,000, to purchase a new plane for him. They told him his skills were too vital for him to not continue working, and he was back at it just two days later.

Morris Harmon, who lived on a farm just north of O'Neill, drove a caterpillar tractor towing a sled. One of his toughest missions was to clear fifty-two miles of road at a speed of about three miles per hour. On the sled, he carried nearly two tons of supplies. This method was deemed a success, and caterpillars towing sleds behind them were sent out in other areas.

The snow was a little lighter in Stuart, Nebraska. Here, a maintainer could work with a crew of about forty or fifty people with shovels. Following them were food and fuel trucks loaded with supplies. Whenever they got close enough to a house for a team and wagon to come out to meet them, they would leave provisions with the family.

As far as getting feed to cattle, members of the Holt County USDA Council considered setting up Operation Haylift. A debate followed, but it was finally decided that using sleds pulled by tractors or trucks following snow-moving equipment was the best course of action. When the army finally arrived with Operation Snowbound on January 29, the equipment they so desperately needed also began to arrive. At first, it was a single bulldozer, which made

Betty, Leroy and Joyce Sporleder at a farm west of Pierce. Nebraskans spent many volunteer hours this winter liberating the snowbound. *Gerald Hixson.*

some question whether they were really going to get the help they were promised. Then came fourteen more.

By February 8, there were 132 bulldozers and several Weasels hard at work in Holt County. They had completed the first phase, which was to clear the main roads within a few miles of every home. Despite the relentless high winds, the workers made good progress with phase two: opening side roads to reach every farmhouse.[84]

For some, being liberated by the snowplows was bittersweet. Dr. David Ikast told the story in the *Lincoln Journal and Star* (now *Lincoln Journal Star*) of how he volunteered his time with a helicopter crew to reach those in need of emergency medical attention. When his aircraft found a family of ten living in the very small village of Verdel, Nebraska, along the northern border of the state not far from Niobrara, he was just in time.

It was bitterly cold when he arrived, with windspeeds as high as thirty-five miles per hour. While many families had canned goods to last them throughout most of their snowbound days, this family was nearly out of everything, from potatoes to the fuel they needed to stay warm. Their two horses had frozen to death just outside of their house, and all they had left were three cows.

The doctor offered to stay while the family evacuated on the helicopter, but they refused to leave their home. They were afraid that if they left, their cows would either freeze to death or starve, and they were not willing to take that chance. It was February 3, and there was no telling how much longer the family would have to remain snowbound. Dr. Ikast and the helicopter crew left food and supplies for the large family and feed for the cows. That was all they could do. The family was grateful.

Not far from this family's home, the doctor and his crew found a bachelor who had also been trapped by the blizzards since November 18. He, too, was grateful for the visitors. He had become so low on fuel that he took a look around his farm and began burning anything he could get his hands on. He was so desperate for fuel that he took up his axe and chopped into his outbuilding.[85]

Dr. Ikast's original intention when heading out with this crew was to check on pregnant mothers and babies with a program he called "Babylift." Somehow, he managed to reach and deliver seventeen babies in twenty days. As far as the number of these babies who were born in a hospital as opposed to those born at home, in a vehicle on the way to the hospital or even in a snowdrift, the ratio was approximately half and half.[86]

Two men make emergency deliveries by plane. When the planes were unable to land, supplies were dropped from the air. *History Nebraska.*

While the air rescue crew was needed to tend to expectant mothers and newborns, Dr. Ikast discovered they were mostly needed to deliver necessities for survival, such as food and fuel. He found another family about twelve miles southwest of Norfolk who had broken up their furniture to burn to keep warm. They had enough food but no oil for their stoves.

These imprisoned people needed supplies and food, but the helicopter crew was also able to get feed to cattle that had been isolated for over a month, and the doctor was able to make house calls. In the Pierce area alone, Dr. Ikast airlifted four patients who were in need of emergency appendectomies.[87]

The winter of 1948–49 was full of misfortunes and obstacles, but those who lived through these blizzards had amazing stories about the good that came out of them, too. In a story from the *Lincoln Journal and Star* written by Stanley A. Matzke, one landowner from Dawson County talked about the cost effectiveness of the windbreaks and shelterbelts planted during the 1930s to counteract the Dust Bowl. Matzke reported: "Thousands of these tree plantings in all parts of the state kept farm yards free of snow drifts and furnished protection for both human and animals from the 40 to 70 mile per hour winds."[88]

Farmers compared stories about their financial losses for years to come, but they were tied to how great the crops were the next year and how green the pastures were with all the extra precipitation brought from the snowmelt. Matzke said that "experts estimated that 160,000 acre feet of water was stored in 6,000 miles of shelterbelts in the state."[89] The snow melted gradually and slowly seeped into the ground, which provided much-needed moisture to the land, and it also helped prevent what some thought would be a terrible spring of flooding rivers throughout the state. Although there was some flooding, it was not as bad as predicted.

As time passed and the anxieties and woes of being cooped up for so long fell away, the recollections of this winter softened into stories about human nature and the kindness of strangers, which reflected the essence of Nebraska's rural communities. The suffering and isolation that characterized this winter did not become as big a part of this story as the acts of heroism and selfless sacrifices that occurred on a regular basis did. People developed a deep appreciation for what they had—things like radios, telephones, electricity, snow-moving equipment and airplanes—including their kind neighbors and caring friends and family.

This sense of optimism is felt even when retelling stories of airlifts that were done for medical emergencies or burning twists of wet hay in the stove because there was nothing left for fuel. Many farmers who met for coffee would talk about the winter lightheartedly, ridiculing the weathermen who certainly did not get the forecasts right this winter. One farmer was quoted as saying: "I'd rather have a warning and no storm than a storm with no warning, I told them. And believe me it really came true on November 18!"[90] They discussed their mishaps, their endless snow scooping and their dwindling coffee and food supplies.

A newspaper correspondent from Royal, Mrs. R.J. Hering, was quoted as saying the following: "City folks just don't believe the stories about the huge snowbanks here. A young lady from the vicinity climbed to the top of a snowbank and sat on the top of a telephone pole, and that isn't a yarn for the liar's club—it is the unvarnished truth."[91]

A rancher from Cherry County who lost track of about three hundred head of cattle but had only fourteen die in the blizzards said, "We're going to have some losses but tell 'em in your headlines that up here in the Sandhills we are going right on raising the finest beef cattle in the world."[92] Near Chadron, rescue crews found eighteen head of cattle that had been covered in snow and ice since January 2. They were not rescued until February 2, and the cows were all still alive.

Cattle, sheep and hog losses were heavy this winter, but they were not as bad as they had originally appeared. Many herds suffocated in the snow or broke though ice-covered waterways and drowned. Some froze to death. Matzke reported: "One farmer found his herd of 60 some head all dead under 15 feet of snow in a canyon into which they had drifted ahead of the storm."[93] Many of these losses, however, were offset by the bountiful crops that were brought in the next year due to the large amount of moisture from the snowmelt.

Some of the losses in the southeastern part of the state were due to a decrease in egg and milk production. This, accompanied by increases in feed costs and the loss of calves, caused an added setback for farmers. It is surprising that optimism remained as high as it did among those who owned livestock, considering the inconveniences and hardships endured for months of isolation during the worst of the winter.

Regarding livestock losses, Matzke wrote that most cattle lost weight. A feedlot in Brown County was unable to provide feed and water to an entire lot full of cows for a week. Even though there were no deaths, it took some extra concentrates and proteins to help the cattle gain back what they had lost. Some cattlemen even said that after being on full feed in the feedlot, the cows were thinner than they had been sixty days prior. Matzke continued:

> *Estimates of livestock deaths were varied, but in view of all available statistics a reasonable guess seemed to be 65,000 head of cattle, 45,000 sheep and 5,000 hogs. Add to the value of these animals the calving and farrowing losses, feed and operation losses, and all other elements directly attributable to the storms and you could, without stretching, establish an overall economic loss approaching $25,000,000 to the state.*[94]

Yet cattlemen did not seem discouraged or have any loss of faith in their operations, and growers, when the spring and summer months brought fields of lush, green crops and pastures, put their energy into looking forward to the abundance they would harvest in the fall. Many landowners had faced rough spots before, and it would take more than one winter for them to show any pessimism.

When the soreness of that winter was finally behind them and they could look to the future, their memories lingered in the stories of the adversities and the fury of the winter that produced blizzard after blizzard, but these were not stories of suffering so much as they were stories of survival.

Other survival stories from this winter centered on the loss of the use of roads and highways. The roads could barely be located, much less cleared of snow for vehicles to get from place to place. It was no wonder there were stories to be told for years to come of the many stranded travelers in Nebraska.

The *Lincoln Journal and Star* said a farm twenty miles northwest of Kimball, on January 2, unexpectedly hosted a number of travelers, as well as a Scottsbluff-Gering bus. The twenty-four passengers sheltered at the farmhouse until help could reach them. A telephone call was placed to Scottsbluff, and plows were soon on their way. Six men and two plows made their way to the farm to rescue these passengers; however, the plows were not able to return due to the drifting snow that had closed the roads behind them. With the rescue attempt unsuccessful, that meant there were now thirty travelers stranded on the farm.

At this point, the other plows had a priority to open Highway 30 across Nebraska to the Wyoming line before they would be able to head north to Kimball, so Mr. and Mrs. Roy Wade did their best to make their thirty guests comfortable until another snowplow could arrive. Knowing these people were imprisoned on the farm, a plow was dispatched as quickly as possible after working on Highway 30. Following it were locals carrying food and provisions for the travelers.

About ten miles north of Kimball in an abandoned house was a young couple who had been traveling through the area and sought shelter wherever they could. They had no food, and the only things they could find for fuel were some pieces of wood and the closest fenceposts they could chop off. They were very happy to see the plow when it came by.

It was not until January 6 that the plow finally made its way to the Wades' farm. The thirty travelers had been well cared for by Mr. and Mrs. Wade, but their food supplies were running quite low. They, too, were very happy to be rescued.[95]

The roads that had been buried so deep for so long encountered quite a bit of damage over this winter. In fact, repairs for the storm-damaged roads in Nebraska went way over budget, costing around $2,500,000 between November 18 and March 1. An average season of repairs would have cost around $250,000, so even though stranded people were rescued, cattlemen's finances recovered and farms turned green, there was no money in the budget for new road construction, and the others were only partially maintained for the rest of 1949.[96]

Some of the survival stories that came out of the blizzards of 1948–49 had a bit of humor to them, showing the lighter side of a serious situation and a realization that Nebraskans would not be defeated, even in their darkest days. The *Lincoln Journal and Star* reported that a class of thirteen students near Gordon had literally been stuck with their teacher for almost a month.

The students and their teacher, Celia Sandoz, had been on a bus on January 19 when they were caught by the storm and unable to continue. The group stumbled onto the Gordon Creek Hereford Ranch, where school continued to be held until they were finally reached by the snowplows and dug out on February 12. They never got to miss a day of school during their confinement, but after that, the students got a much-deserved winter break.

There is another story of a bulldozer crew that reached a ranch north of Stuart. As the driver was clearing the lane and access trails around the farm, he suggested he clear a path to the nearest haystack. The seventy-five-year-old rancher insisted the bulldozer make a path to the haystack nearly two miles away. He said he was saving these closer ones for "bad weather."

Leonard Juracek of O'Neill was reminded of the blizzard of '49 every time he used his six hundred feet of garden hoses. Two of his wells had frozen, but he still had water from the well that supplied his house. He had an idea to get enough hose to run a line from the house to the stock tanks, so he ordered two hundred feet of hose. With the storm delaying the delivery of his order, the Red Cross showed up at his place with an emergency delivery of two hundred feet of hose. He was very grateful to them for their efforts, but not long after that, he received the delivery of his original shipment by ski plane, and he found himself with another two hundred feet of hose. This happened just as a helpful neighbor carried over yet another two hundred feet of hose.

The very small community of Flats (with a population of eight in 1940) asked Governor Val Peterson if the Internal Revenue Service would allow them a "stay of execution," since they were clearly snowbound and would be unable to file their income taxes before the deadline.

Ray A. Dyke, a meteorologist at the Lincoln Weather Bureau (now the National Weather Service), while speaking to members of the January 12, 1888 Blizzard Club was quoted as saying: "In strength of wind, amount of snow, and duration of weather conditions, the January 3-5, 1949, blizzard was the worst that ever visited Nebraska." Not to let down club members, however, he added that the Great Blizzard of 1888 had a bit of an advantage in low temperatures and in covering a larger area.

A farm family near Crawford, who had lots of chickens, was just sitting down to yet another breakfast of eggs when the bulldozer finally arrived at their place. The family was happy to feed the men a hearty egg breakfast. With so many chickens and nowhere to deliver their produce, the family had filled every basket and container they could find with eggs, but the chickens keep laying. The bulldozer crew found another eighty dozen eggs or so carefully piled in the kitchen.

At the Charley Cronk farm near Taylor, arrangements had been made for several bales of hay to be dropped by air on February 4. Shortly after the C-47 took off, the crew noticed a peculiar yet distinct odor coming from one of the bales. When the flight reached its drop zone, not knowing which bale of hay held the foul-smelling, air-lifted creature, the Cronk farm received fifty bales of hay and one skunk.[97]

Slowly but surely, Operation Snowbound made headway against the snow-plugged country roads and highways. One by one, the bulldozers and snowplows were able to keep up with the drifting. Through trial and error, the right plowing techniques minimized the drifting, and traffic began to flow again. While travel was certainly not as smooth as it would normally be in good weather, the situation was better than it had been in late January 1949. By mid-February, not warm but moderate temperatures caused existing snow piles to melt slowly, which mercifully caused the snowing and drifting to end temporarily, allowing snowplowing crews to really put a dent in the snow-covered landscape.

5

OPERATION SNOWBOUND WRAPS UP

ike any military operation, General Pick's Operation Snowbound eventually came to a close. Their enemy this time was not an army of thousands with machine guns, tanks and artillery pieces; it was Mother Nature herself, a formidable enemy. Subzero, wind-driven cold air can kill just as surely as a bullet.

Throughout the road-clearing project, the little Weasels clanked and scurried across the deep snow where no other equipment could go, delivering supplies to each farmhouse in the area. Wherever they went, the drivers found people grateful for their help who were willing to lend a hand of their own. Many of the Weasel and bulldozer drivers were not locals, so Operation Snowbound progressed into a coordinated effort, with some locals helping by knowing how to run the equipment and some helping by being more familiar with the land.

As much attention had been given to the people who went above and beyond the call of duty, the blizzards had also made some of the snow-moving equipment heroes and heroines in their own right. John Koffend wrote about Henriette, "the 14-ton lady from Kansas City," in an article for the *Omaha World-Herald*:

> *She was born a working girl, an earth-mover, a digger of basements and an uprooter of trees. What's glamorous or heroic about a yellow tractor with a three-foot exhaust pipe and an insatiable appetite for oil? Well, just ask the people of Sargent for the answer to that. Henriette had her shining hour,*

all right. And when lists are drawn of those who fought and conquered the snow, Henriette's name will be near the top. The morning she hit town, perched high and mighty on her trailer, she'd already come five hundred miles to the battlefront. The going had been weary and slow; now and then Henriette had had to crawl down and widen the road for the big truck which carried her....Some of the snowbound folks gathered round to give Henriette the eye, but much as she loved the attention, she had no time for it. There was work to do. Beneath her yellow hood slept 65 horses. And until her boss, Howard Saferite, lashed them into thundering life and sent her charging at the white enemy imprisoning the land, Henriette was no more than a hunk of steel. But in action she was something to behold...and Henriette lumbered eagerly away. Eight miles down the Middle Loup River Road, behind drifts unchallenged for more than a month, a farm family named Steggall awaited the stork. This was a mission worthy of Henriette, and she plunged to it with cocksure will.[98]

Henriette's boss, Howard Saferite, was proud of his "girl" and boasted about how she could push the snow around with her Caterpillar muscles better than any of the others. Occasionally, she did get stuck in the deep snowdrifts, but she always struggled loose. Saferite said that this storm brought more snow with it than he had ever seen before, but his girl would not let them down.

Henriette worked day and night, spotted by two drivers working twelve-hour shifts, seven days a week. Koffend wrote: "Henriette was made for toil, and once she growled into action, she didn't stop until the job was done. The snow was tough, but Henriette was tougher. Inch by inch, yard by yard, she stole back the captive roads."[99]

It was true that Henriette was admired by those along her route; in fact, many liberated farmers came out to applaud her work, bringing hot coffee and food to her drivers or jumping on board to guide them around the buildings on the farm, to haystacks in the fields and across bridges on the roads.

Henriette was a fine lady indeed, but her spotlight was stolen part of the time by the work of a Weasel named Flo. Like the new girl in town, the boys to turn their heads in Flo's direction whenever they heard the sweet music of her motor clattering its way onto their farms. They were impressed with the agile way she climbed right over the snowdrifts without breaking through the crust like the heavier equipment did.

Although Flo stole a bit of the limelight from Henriette, carrying supplies to snowbound farmhouses, Henriette's talent for road clearing with a tireless energy was not surpassed. There was no rust found on her steel tracks, and her big mechanical heart pumped strongly, pushing her eight-foot blade deeper and deeper into mountains of snow.

The local group of disaster committee volunteers in Sargent kept track of Henriette's advancement. She was quite the heroine. By her second day, she had freed seven farm families, including the town doctor. Altogether, during her brief visit, she dug out more than forty-five families before pressing on to the next combat zone to continue her fight in the war against the blizzards.

The personification of the equipment that liberated people this winter was probably more common than one would think. After all, the maintainers, bulldozers and tractors worked everywhere, all across the whiteness that covered the land. When they cleared a path through the snow, they were literally lifesavers to people and animals. Koffend wrote:

> *Then one day Henriette would be back in Kansas City, back to the prosaic tasks of a tractor designed for pushing old Mother Earth around. But for a few brief weeks she and the other bulldozers that came north and the crews that manned them had done heroic work. And all Nebraska knew it.*[100]

By February 13, the army began transferring Weasels from the improving weather situation in Nebraska to the still nightmarish situation in North Dakota. Before long, the bulldozers began to leave areas in the north-central part of the state. By February 19, more counties in the panhandle were demobilized as Operation Snowbound was winding down toward the end of February.

As anyone could imagine, there were criticisms of Operation Snowbound. Some of these centered on the early snow-clearing work, because snowplows were focusing on certain priorities over others. Some said that "army red tape" prevented work from being done as fast as they would have liked. Others grumbled about damages to their property due to the bulldozers not being able to see objects underneath the snowbanks.[101]

However, most Nebraskans supported and praised Operation Snowbound and the efforts of the military. Most of the time, when military personnel arrived on a rural property, farmers and ranchers were grateful for their efforts and received them warmly. Not to mention, the soldiers were usually given all the hot food and coffee they could eat or drink.

The work these men encountered on the ground sometimes had its pitfalls—literally. One army sergeant, posted in Mullen, accidentally walked through the wrong door at a local café and fell into a basement. The fall killed

Two men stand by a bulldozer. These machines did not have canopies, making it hazardous for the drivers during extreme winter conditions. *Gerald Hixson.*

the man, who was a decorated World War II veteran and had, ironically, managed to survive the war but not Operation Snowbound.

Nebraskans prided themselves on being self-sufficient, especially during the Great Depression and the Dust Bowl, so this current program of help from the federal government tested the pride of most people in the state. By the end of January, however, personal pride gave way to the reality of the snowdrifts that threatened the economy and the lives of Nebraskans.

From the very beginning of Operation Snowbound, General Pick made it crystal clear that the Fifth Army would be engaging in total war against the elements. He knew that the daily reports he gave about the miles of roads cleared and the numbers of livestock and people dug out would boost morale and were not unlike news reports of Allied forces advancing in the last months of fighting in the European theater during World War II.

Nebraskans were impressed by the common sense, can-do attitude of the general who solved a problem that they grudgingly admitted could not be overcome by themselves. Through it all, the operation ran its course to completion, with its final demobilization on March 15. At the operation's peak, around February 9–10, the amount of personnel working in the care of Operation Snowbound was counted as 6,237. According to Dalstrom:

This figure included 4,008 private contract workers, eighteen employees of the National Red Cross, and 959 civil service employees of the Missouri River Division of the Army Corps of Engineers. In sum, Operation Snowbound employed a maximum of 4,985 civilians. At this point, 1,252 members of the armed forces were assigned to Operation Snowbound. Their numbers included 807 from the Army; 293 from the Air Force; 136 members of the National Guard; and 16 in the Navy. Of course, additional people were under Operation Snowbound command at other times. For example, the total naval contingent included 35 persons, and, as noted earlier, some 250 members of the Nebraska National Guard were on duty in early February.[102]

Operation Snowbound was an immense undertaking with jaw-dropping statistics. The entire enterprise spanned 193,193 square miles across four states. For an engagement that lasted six weeks, 6,000 men and 1,600 pieces of equipment were used to clear 115,138 miles of road and save 4,011,184 cattle from certain death and 243,780 people from being trapped in their homes.[103]

When demobilization finally took place and most areas in Nebraska had been freed, it was estimated that the entire zone affected by the devastating snows in the Dakotas, Wyoming, Colorado and Nebraska was an area nearly the size of France.

6

KEEPING THE TRAINS MOVING

U nlike clearing highways and country roads, keeping railroad tracks cleared of snow was a different animal entirely. Train crews basically had three options for plowing through snowdrifts blocking the right of way, and none of them were ideal.

One device used was the wedge plow, which looked like an overgrown plow that farmers use to till their soil, which was attached to the front of the locomotive and then used to push snow to each side, like the plows used on trucks then as well as today. The plow was connected to a ballast car that was placed in front of the train and used for transporting coal and other necessities that the crew would need for their journey.

The ballast car gave the locomotive the necessary momentum and mass needed to break through the enormous snowdrifts. A train utilizing the wedge plow had to collide with drifts at a very high speed to punch through them—at least fifty miles per hour—which was extremely hazardous, because by hitting a snowbank that fast, the crew ran the risk of derailing the train. Another problem was that the wedge plow did not push the snow far enough away from the track. Miles-long ridges of snow would pile up alongside the tracks, turning them into trenches that the blowing snow could easily fill in.

A second type of plow used to remove snow from the railways was the rotary plow. It traveled at a much slower speed, but it could devour drifts much larger than any wedge plow ever could. The rotary plow was a lot safer to operate, since it moved at a slower speed, but it was also a lot more expensive to run than a wedge plow, because it required an entire railroad crew to maintain and drive it. With this plow, a steam locomotive was used to power a spinning blade that threw snow away from the tracks, much like a snow blower does when used to clean off a driveway after a blizzard.

A third, but extremely dangerous snow-removal technique was the use of dynamite, but this was to be used as a last resort. Sure, it could obliterate a snowdrift in a second, but dynamite can be extremely dangerous. The ill-timed detonation of a stick of dynamite in too close proximity to a worker could result in the loss of limbs or, worse, life.

The railroads definitely saw their share of difficulties due to the heavy snowfall and deep drifts. Every line going east–west, except one, was blocked due to snow, and every track going north was closed. Trains were stopped, and the snowplows sent in as rescue vehicles were stuck and became buried in drifts as high as their smokestacks. The wind blew drifting snow across railroad lines and roads as soon as they were opened. Smith reported:

> *Some 7,500 passengers on 50 trains were backed up as far as Pocatello, and Salt Lake City to the west and to Chicago on the east.…The Burlington had a bad nightmare with its passenger train at Seneca. The steam pipes of the stalled train froze. Snow blown into coach vestibules and tracked through the train melted into puddles and then froze. Passengers made their way to the depot and then to a café where they were jampacked for 24 hours until the arrival of a plow and relief train carrying an oxygen tent for a passenger ill with pneumonia. The Northwestern found itself faced with a snow barricade, ranged in depth up to 30 feet, stretching one hundred miles west from Cody. Rotary after rotary went against the snow only to be derailed or smashed. The snow packed so densely that dynamite was used to blast it open. Measuring progress in inches, workers still had not opened the blockade two weeks after the storm.*[104]

The winter of 1948–49 was one of the worst in the history of Nebraska railroads. The clearing of the Burlington's Ashby Cut, between Hyannis and Alliance, soon became a legendary tale known as "The Battle of the Cut."[105]

The raging winds and heavy snow that had swept across the hills for the last fifteen hours had settled itself deeply in this particular cut where the railroad passed through. This was part of the line from Lincoln to Billings that crews were diligently working to get opened as quickly as possible. The story goes that a train began traveling west out of Hyannis on January 3, and when it reached the three-thousand-foot cut near Ashby, the snow edged high above the engines, and the train was not able to get through.

These train tracks outside of Gordon are flanked by towering snowbanks. Sometimes, dynamite was used to blast through ice-covered snowdrifts. *History Nebraska.*

This artery was an important transportation route across the country, and many people were counting on the line being reopened, so the men backed up the plow and took another run at it. The two hefty engines behind the plow pushed and pushed, ramming it deeper into the white abyss. They continued their efforts until the engine overheated, gave a heavy sigh and stopped.

Just then, another sound smothered the fading train whistle as a forty-foot wall of snow plummeted down on the engines. For the next ninety-six hours, in subzero temperatures, workers exhausted themselves with the grueling task of frantically shoveling mountains of snow from the train to free the engineers and firemen trapped inside the locomotives, snowplow and coal car underneath all that snow.

As the stalled engines cooled, they melted the snow around them, creating an ice-covered, snow-clad iron horse. Emergency crews worked around the clock to get to the men, dig out the train and open the track. They reached the rear engine within forty-eight hours, but the Battle of the Cut continued for four straight days until January 7, when the snowplow was finally released from its trap.[106]

Burlington representatives said that this winter was the worst on record for its duration, severity, far-reaching expanse and cost, but the Burlington was not the only railroad to run into brutal winter difficulties. There were 15 rotary plows in use by the Union Pacific and 33 wedge plows. In addition to these, the railroad had 180 bulldozers and 124 flame throwers. Some fourteen thousand employees battled the snow and ice day after day. The onslaught continued for seven weeks in temperatures that were well below freezing, with winds reaching up to eighty miles per hour.[107]

On January 18, a Union Pacific plow skimmed off the tracks due to ice-covered drifts that covered the line, and the plow came back around and crashed into the train, cropping the sides off two locomotives. This was quite a predicament, as the line was still blocked with ice and snow, and the engines were a mangled pile of debris. Workers struggled for eight hours with acetylene torches to reach the trainman who was still inside the twisted wreckage. Unfortunately, they were too late, and the man died at the scene.

Crews with the Chicago and North Western labored for days on end in the northern part of Nebraska. The exhausted men scooped all day to excavate the buried tracks but could clear only a few feet by dark, and repeatedly, when light appeared the next morning, the tracks would be filled in again by the unyielding, blowing and drifting snow. Maintaining the lines was a hopeless task, and these trains were not going anywhere.

Frank Stempek of Duncan on a Big Boy locomotive. These locomotives articulated in the middle, allowing them to bend around curves. *Platte County Historical Society.*

Although some trains were snowbound, other lines remained open or partially open, even playing their part in mercy missions. When a plane that was heading to Alliance with a sick patient was attempting to take off from a ranch near Antioch, it nosed over and injured both the patient and the pilot.

Luckily, a snowplow with the Burlington was able to pick up both of them and deliver them safely to Alliance.

A settlement of French families who lived eighteen miles from Crawford in Nebraska's panhandle found themselves crucially low on food and fuel and sent a man to walk the entire distance to the small town. In Crawford, the man was able to secure twelve tons of food and supplies for the village to be delivered by train at a point four miles east of Joder. The trainmen even helped unload the supplies for the grateful people.[108]

Travel delays are bad enough under normal circumstances, but the passengers aboard the Union Pacific train that left Lincoln on January 2, 1949, bound for Chadron, ended up suspending their trips for quite some time. What should have been a comfortable traveling experience aboard the train turned into a story of survival, one about making the most of unexpected circumstances and how easy it can be for plans to fall apart.

Although it was the middle of winter when the train left Lincoln, no one expected to see snow heavy enough to stop a locomotive. They were nearly halfway to their destination when the travelers found themselves in the middle of the worst of the storm. Still, no one was too worried until the lights went out and the steam pipes froze.

Snow came into the coaches, melted and turned to ice. The freezing passengers were stranded near Anselmo, but the railroad crew cleared the tracks little by little and slowly lumbered forward for the next sixty miles of the trip until they reached Seneca, which had a population of about 250 people. There the train stopped and waited for the rest of the line to be cleared to Chadron.[109]

By this time, the passengers were freezing, huddled under every available blanket. After ten hours of waiting in the cold train at Seneca, another engine appeared and attempted to save the day by attaching its flexible steam pipes to those on the stranded train to try to get some heat to the passengers. Their efforts were unsuccessful.

The frigid conditions became too intolerable for the passengers, and remaining on board the train was no longer an option. Some of the women and children had to be carried from the cars, through the blizzard and into the depot, as the conditions had become so miserable. At last, the displaced passengers thought there would be some relief from the biting cold, but that was not to be the case. Just as they walked into the depot, the fire in the stove burned out, and there was no fuel to get it going again. Their luck took a turn of sorts when they were able to seek shelter at a nearby café.

Union Pacific Railroad crews work to free stranded trains after the blizzard. Many Nebraskans depended on trains for their livelihoods. *History Nebraska.*

The café may have provided shelter, but it was barely big enough to fit everyone inside. Some, many of them children, slept on tabletops, while others lay on the hard floor. There was not enough room for everyone to stretch out on the floor and there were not enough chairs to sit on either, so the rest of the group took turns standing and sitting. The only bathroom was outside, so a burst of cold air blasted through the small café whenever the door was opened.

The village of Seneca was able to get hot meals to the passengers, so at least nobody went hungry. It was not until Tuesday, two days after the passengers had left Lincoln, that another train was able to collect most of the passengers for a return trip to Lincoln.

About thirty passengers remained in Seneca, still intending to get to Chadron. These people were able to walk over to the heated school, which at least had indoor plumbing. They camped out in the gymnasium, played basketball, told stories and sang songs around the piano until they could continue on their way. Nearly a week after they left Lincoln, at 3:30 a.m. on January 9, these travelers were finally able to board another train heading west to their destination.[110] Did they ever have a story to tell to those who had been eagerly awaiting their arrival in Chadron.

From a letter by William W. Adams of Kansas City, Kansas, a passenger aboard the Burlington train stranded at Seneca:

The train stopped the following morning at 3 o'clock. There we sat for nearly 12 hours, away from everything but snow—rolling, drifting snow. Then, in less than three hours, we crawled thru snow tunnels cut in drifts above the car windows, 60 miles to Seneca, Neb., a village of 250 people, and 478 miles from Kansas City. It was then after 5 o'clock in the afternoon of Monday, Jan. 3.

In about an hour, our lights died and train began to grow cold. The conductor informed us that the steam rods underneath the train had frozen! Faithful trainmen sought vainly to reopen the frozen pipes, until their faces froze! Then they gave it up!

Finally the order was given to abandon the train. This in the midst of the worst blizzard know in Nebraska history! The air was filled with blinding snow, whipped by a 60-mile wind (official, not a guess) in a sub-zero temperature and with snow drifts up to 25 feet deep.

Fortunately the train's engine had stopped about 100 yards from the depot, on the one side and from Ruby's Café, on the other. All passengers were ordered to move ahead and to detrain from the forward coach. Then by keeping close to the remaining cars and engines, on the leeward side, the women could walk alone. But beyond the engine, in the open space of 100 yards leading to the "harbors of safety," we had to steady the women to keep them on their feet and to shield their faces so that they could breathe.

By 7 o'clock Tuesday night, the rotary snow plow from the east arrived, bringing medical supplies, including an oxygen tent for our pneumonia patient, Orville Miller, of Lincoln. At 11:45 with the blizzard blasting *away its 55th hour in full fury, our train started back east, with all the passengers that could be crowded into the rear Pullman car, the only one in which people could ride and live. By 4:35 in the morning, we had gone the 82 miles to Broken Bow, where we placed Orville Miller in an ambulance to be carried to the hospital.*[111]

Around this same time, another passenger train, the *City of San Francisco*, got stuck with its 270 passengers just outside of Kimball, twenty miles from Pine Bluffs, Wyoming. The temperature was negative four degrees Fahrenheit, the wind gusts reached speeds up to sixty miles per hour and the visibility was about thirty feet.[112] With these conditions, along with the heavy snow, the engineer made the decision to stop the train and head back toward his best estimate of where the Kimball depot was located.

Since the depot had reported the train as leaving Kimball but it did not show up in Pine Bluffs, reporters began to question its whereabouts. Art Henrickson at Kimball's newspaper office soon received a phone call from *Life* magazine inquiring about the train. Henrickson fought his way through the blizzard to the depot, where he found the train along the north side of the building. The storm was so severe that the people working at the station did not even realize the train had backed up and was sitting just outside their depot.

The newspaperman boarded the train to check on the passengers, who were doing fine at the time. He was led around by an older man, who would not give his name, and introduced to the passengers. He then took photographs and asked them about their travels. Henrickson also took pictures of the snowbound train and then slowly proceeded back to his office, where he made a return phone call to *Life* magazine. They definitely wanted his photographs.

Although Kimball was several times larger than Seneca, it looked like the *City of San Francisco* would remain where it was until the storm subsided. It was not long before its steam pipes froze, as they had on the Seneca train, and there was no heat left to warm the passengers. Another steam engine from Sidney showed up the next day to do what it could to heat the stranded train, but it, too, soon became frozen, and the passengers had to disembark.

The train crew helped all 270 passengers over to the two hotels in town, the Kimball Hotel and the Wheat Growers Hotel, but there were not enough accommodations for everyone. People slept wherever they could find a spot, rotating the use of the beds with night and day shifts. For food, the Kimball Café was open around the clock. Even though the hotel dining room was closed, the staff from the train brought it back to life and were able to serve hot meals there.

Some of the passengers stayed in private homes, and a few of them even rented a house for their unplanned visit to Kimball. According to Dalstrom:

> *On the evening of January 5 a passenger, A. Perry Osborn, first vice president of the American Museum of Natural History in New York, reportedly phoned his secretary and complained that the train crew had essentially left the passengers to fend for themselves. Osborn was especially anxious because he could not secure an estimated arrival time in San Francisco. His secretary passed the complaint to the Union Pacific corporate headquarters in New York, which forwarded the gist of the complaint to the Omaha office of George F. Ashby, the railroad's president. Ashby himself was stranded aboard a Union Pacific train in Cheyenne, but A.J. Seltz, Union Pacific vice president of traffic, phoned Osborn in Kimball. Osborn now put a more positive light on the situation, saying that some crewmembers had been helpful, and that a passenger agent had given him useful information.… The following month, E. Roland Harriman, chairman of the Union Pacific Board of Directors, wrote to congratulate Perry Osborn saying, "I have seen several of your co-passengers and some of the operating men all of whom reported to the same effect, that your common sense and initiative were of great value in the emergency." Harriman told Seitz, "I learned at first hand in San Francisco that he [Osborn] had been very helpful with the passengers and I thought it appropriate to acknowledge it."[113]*

Meanwhile, Art Henrickson from the *Western Nebraska Observer* made another trip back to the depot to see if he could find more information about the old man who had introduced him to the passengers on board the train and encouraged him to take the photographs for *Life* magazine. It turned out that the man was actually the father of Henry Luce, the man who founded *Time* and *Life* magazines.

Drifts up to thirty feet high remained on the tracks between Sidney and Cheyenne, but the Union Pacific was able to open an alternate route across northern Colorado to Laramie, Wyoming, and the *City of San Francisco* was on its way. The article that later appeared in *Life*, along with Art Hendrickson's photographs, made the sojourn of the train and of the passengers at Kimball another story of survival to be shared for years to come.[114]

Another story tells of the train crew in Ravenna, whose plan was to travel through the Sandhills to Alliance, about 240 miles to the west. Even though

Union Pacific employee Frank Stempek watches a train with a rotary plow clear snow away from a track. *Platte County Historical Society.*

they were aware of the dropping temperatures and the potential for drifting to occur on the tracks between the hills in this part of central Nebraska, the train engineer John Rogers convinced those in Alliance who were advising against travel that he could make the trip.[115]

The weather was clear in Ravenna when they departed on January 2, and the temperature was around fifteen degrees, which was quite a bit cooler than the sixty degrees they had enjoyed the day before. But it did not seem possible that they would soon find themselves in the middle of the worst battle between snow and steel that they had ever encountered. Not long after the train, with its thirty-three passengers, began its journey, the temperature dropped even lower, and the snow started to fall. The wind picked up speed, and in no time, the crew experienced low visibility, with snow accumulating across the tracks.

The train stopped about fifty miles into the trip so the crew could restock coal bins and water tanks. When they continued, the drifts became deeper, about three feet high. Their next stop was Anselmo. Here, Rogers called ahead to Alliance to see if the weather conditions had improved. They had not. The temperature was now negative fifteen degrees Fahrenheit, and no trains were moving. The engineer's train had no plow, but he still felt confident he could break through the drifts and make it to Alliance.

They continued to push through heaps of snow until they reached Halsey. They stopped at the depot to replenish the coal and water and check once again on conditions up ahead. Rogers learned that all the trains coming from the west had stopped, most with frozen pipes, and the passengers had to leave the trains to find other shelter.

With his train about three hours behind, the engineer was determined to push on toward Alliance, even though snow accumulations were creating larger obstructions across the tracks. Rogers noted that whenever he saw drifting, he opened the throttle and smashed into the snow at about fifty miles per hour. Each time he did this, he could feel the impact of the locomotive breaking through.

The weather continued to worsen, with snow accumulating in larger quantities and for longer distances. Even though Rogers hit the snowdrifts at fifty miles per hour, he was barely moving by the time the train cleared them. They were now running five hours late, but they were still moving west.

Soon, the train was crashing through drifts that were ten to fifteen feet deep and as long as a quarter of a mile. In Whitman, which was about seventy miles outside of Alliance, the temperature was negative twenty-eight degrees Fahrenheit, and theirs was the only train still moving. Then they came upon the largest drift they had encountered so far.

Rogers opened the throttle and blasted into the snow with the mighty strength of the locomotive. The crew was thrust forward with the collision, and quite possibly, everyone on board thought this was the place where they would have to stop. It felt as though the train would derail. The wheels spun on the tracks, but they kept moving, inching forward little by little until they cleared the barrier and started to gain speed again for the last leg of the journey.

The train was only fifty miles from Alliance when the water tank for the steam engine froze up. The crew was unsure if there would be enough pressure to make it the rest of the way, especially with the enormous mounds of snow they were crashing into at top speed, which slowed them down significantly each time.

At the Lakeside depot, only twenty miles from Alliance, the red board was put out, indicating the train had to stop. The Alliance depot told the train to stay there, that the tracks were impassible from Lakeside to Alliance, but Rogers claimed that he had made it this far by crashing through the drifts at full speed and that he could make it the last twenty miles the same

A Union Pacific train with a rotary plow blows a plume of snow away from a stranded locomotive. *Platte County Historical Society.*

way. The Alliance manager agreed to the determined engineer's request to continue, and Rogers climbed into the locomotive again; however, the train would not move.

There was so much frozen snow and ice packed under the train that it was nearly frozen in place. Rogers pulled the throttle forward and back, rocking the train loose, and soon, he pulled away from the Lakeside depot. The drifts along the last few miles of their trek did not get any smaller and actually grew in size. The train finally met its match when it ran into a fifteen-foot drift. It could go no farther.

The train had slowed and did not have the momentum to punch through this drift like it had through the others. Finally, it came to a compete stop. It was out of water, freezing and its undercarriage was packed with ice. The train was only one hundred yards from the Alliance depot, but it would be another two weeks before trains in this area were able to move again.[116]

Many railroads had to shut down, as they just could not buck the drifts. Derailments occurred several times during the brutal storms. In Page, just east of O'Neill, a snowplow and two train engines were thrown off the tracks on December 29. The rescue plow that was sent out on January 2 became cut off and unable to assist. The equipment and train engines were soon drifted over with snow. It was not until February 22 that the engines were restored and this line of the Burlington was finally reopened.

In the meantime, the citizens of Nebraska had to make do with the situation as best as they could. There was not a real end to the winter nightmare until the sustained spring thaws of April arrived to melt the icy hellscape. Until then, it was the life of cabin fever.

KILLING TIME AND KEEPING SANE
WHEN SNOWBOUND

I t would be hard for us in the twenty-first century to imagine life without television, internet, videogames, smartphones or electricity, but that is the way things were for some people in the winter of 1948–49. Imagine spending hours and days on end without a screen of some kind to look at, with nothing more than walls and windows to stare at. Wait, we could talk to our friends and family members in something called a *conversation* and engage in something called reading a book. Sorry for the sarcasm, but the experiences of people in the late 1940s that we would find so foreign today was just normal life to our grandparents.

The truth of surviving the winter of 1948–49 was mostly the day-to-day business of staying alive: making sure the kitchen pantry was stocked with food; having an ample supply of coal and wood to keep the house heated; filling in those cracks in the walls with caulk, plaster, mud or whatever was available to keep the house insulated; and, lastly, maintaining mental health. It was important to find something stimulating for the brain, be it reading, playing cards or just taking part in a good old-fashioned conversation.

Most farmhouses at that time had a summer kitchen and a winter kitchen. The summer kitchen was an attached room on one side of the house to keep the warmth from the stove from overheating the house during the stifling summer months of Nebraska. The winter kitchen was located at the center of the house on the ground level so its stove could serve the dual purpose of cooking and providing heating for the house during the frigid winter months.

Most stoves at the time could accommodate the burning of both wood and coal. Coal was ready for the stove the moment it was delivered; wood, on the other hand, needed a long preparation time before it could be burned. As all country folks know, after a piece of wood is cut, it needs to dry out in a woodshed for a year. A freshly cut piece of wood is too green to burn.

Typically, a woodshed contains two piles of wood: the freshly cut pile, which must sit for a year to dry out properly, and the old pile, with wood pieces that were cut a year before and are now ready for the fireplace. Wood cutting season typically started at the end of October with the end of the harvest and would ideally need to be finished before Thanksgiving, when the first snowfall and severe cold usually arrived. The key word here is *usually*. (As any lifelong Nebraskan knows, we can get snow, ice or freezing temperatures anytime between early October and early May.)

Those who failed to have an adequate supply of coal and firewood were forced to burn anything they could to stay warm and cook their next meal. Imagine the heartbreak of having to chop up an old family heirloom, like an antique treasure chest or dresser, into pieces and throw it into the fireplace just to keep warm for another day. Or think of how painful it would feel for a family to have to pry off a wooden piece of their own house and use that as firewood. Life-or-death decisions like this had to be made every day that winter.

Another persistent problem with poor insulation in the winter was the constant sweeping of snow from the floor, especially the floors of attics under old roofs. Yes, that is correct. Just like dusting is an endless chore in any house year-round, sweeping up snow was a necessary task during this winter—or any severe winter for that matter. The attic is often the room that is ignored the most in any household, but to do this would have risked disaster during that winter in particular. There could be big trouble if, for example, an attic went unattended for a month, from Christmas to the end of January. Slowly, but surely, snowflakes falling through the cracks of an old roof would accumulate and form a heavy pile on the attic floor, pushing against and rotting the wood.[117] If left unchecked, this could rot out a portion of the ceiling in any room directly under the attic, eventually collapsing it and leaving the homeowner with a massive repair job and bill.

Nebraskans who planned for the long, cold winter months ahead often spent their summers canning garden produce. Almost every farm that did not have electricity had a cellar or root cellar. This was an area often accessible from outside the house that was dug into the ground as a cool place to store food. It also kept the food from freezing and stopped animals from getting into it. (It doubled as a tornado shelter in the spring and summer.)

Items such as carrots, sweet potatoes, onions, squash, apples and regular potatoes were often found in root cellars because they were easy to pick and place in there without much preparation. They usually kept for a relatively long period without spoiling in this cool, dark place. Sometimes, fruits were dried and placed in these cellars along with jars of jelly and other preserved foods.[118]

With the ability to go to a grocery store being unpredictable at best and impossible at worst, the craft of canning perishables in jars during the summer and fall was an absolute lifesaver for the hearty souls of rural Nebraska. This involved putting fruits and vegetables into glass jars, placing a metal cover on top with a wax seal around the edge and fastening it into place with a ringed washer. The final part of canning involved submerging six or seven of the jars in a kettle filled with boiling water. This caused the wax to partially melt, creating the airtight seal that preserved the canned foods for months or even years, providing meal after meal of nourishing food at home when travel to replenish supplies was difficult to impossible.

With doctors and hospitals unable to be reached for days or even weeks at a time during this winter, people had to know a bit about first-aid and maybe some common folk remedies as well: honey for a cough, chili peppers for sore joints and a good bowl of chicken noodle soup for a cold. Women also had to help each other if the stork decided to make a delivery in the depths of this winter.

As for rural farm kids, their biggest adjustment was missing school for weeks or, in certain cases, months at a time. Some teachers adjusted by giving out their assignments by phone. This made the party line setup quite convenient. Teachers could make one phone call and have all of their students listen in at the same time, or better yet, they could conduct an entire lecture via a phone call. Others made the decision to mail the assignments to their students.

Some parents had the novel idea of bringing their children's teacher to them to have them conduct school in their own home. Some teachers even lived in their students' homes until the weather improved. A few teachers, on the other hand, took advantage of the situation and tried their best not to make the trip to school, even if conditions moderated enough to permit safe passage there and back.

School district superintendents ruled that extended school closures due to the weather were the legal equivalent of closures due to epidemic outbreaks, so teachers were paid the same salary without having to make up the school days lost. Those same superintendents, however, were peppered with complaints that some teachers and students were indeed abusing the situation and missing school time that they should not have. Various school districts reached a compromise, which let individual school boards decide whether teachers would take a cut in pay or be forced into making up the lost school days at a later date.[119]

Last but not least, maintaining mental health during these many months of boredom and isolation was key. Favorite pastimes among the World War II generation were the many varieties of card games. Whether they were played as friendly competitions among friends or at cards clubs or parties, the favorite games were poker, pitch, rummy, pinochle and blackjack. Card playing provided hours of free and fun entertainment for everyone, although some games were known to take an unexpected turn and grow into a new game called "fifty-two-card pickup." Other popular games included checkers, marbles, jacks and board games like *Monopoly* and *Chutes and Ladders*. Sometimes, a chalkboard or a slate and chalk could be used to play games or create drawings.

Another favorite pastime was reading, either silently or aloud and to the children, even if the stories were old familiar ones. There was music if anyone

A dog happily runs across a snowbank. Pets got lots of attention during the long weeks of being snowbound. *Gerald Hixson.*

in the household played an instrument, and there was always cooking and sewing to keep busy. There was also the good old-fashioned act of having a conversation with friends and family to calm the senses. Eventually, the month of February drew to a close, and the severity of this winter subsided.

By mid-February, enough progress had been made in the plowing of country roads that things began to open up again. If any family was still snowbound at this time, they did not have long to wait until they were freed.[120] The snow emergency was finally coming to an end, and any feelings of helplessness or of being isolated were quickly tossed aside.

Most residents were quite proud of how effectively they had "weathered the storm." There were countless people who stepped up to help others during this winter. Nebraskans everywhere showed a certain amount of determination that would not let them see the storms that blanketed the area as an enemy that pinned them down; instead they saw them as an obstacle to overcome. They kept their minds on the tasks at hand day by day, yet they kept their eyes looking forward to better times and warmer weather.

Of course, being snowbound, for many people, had not been about lazily sitting around reading and eating. Aside from working to provide basic needs, large numbers of people volunteered to help in any way possible, from answering emergency calls and checking with neighbors to opening and reopening miles and miles of roads. Crews of bulldozer and snowplow drivers worked long shifts, helped by local guides and fed by local farm families. Weasels popped up around the rural communities, taking supplies and information back and forth. People volunteered with helicopter crews and small planes, airlifting supplies and making emergency landings in the bitterly cold winds. Although the blizzards had cut people off, they had also, surprisingly, brought people together in a coordinated effort to defeat a common enemy.

For families who had been trapped since before Christmas, they were more than ready to give up their days of volunteering or working around the farm just to try to keep up with the necessities of life. With the roads finally becoming clear enough to use, it was time to go to town, visit the grocery stores, catch up with people and start going to card clubs and get-togethers again.

With time marching on and the knowledge that spring would bring warmer weather, Nebraska would soon have another problem to contend with: the spring rains and melting snow that could cause flooding. This led some to speculate if "Operation Flood-bound" was looming.

8

LATE FEBRUARY AND MARCH
MELTDOWN AND DIG-OUT

By late February and early March 1949, the temperatures had moderated enough to allow snow-clearing crews to get ahead for once. Winter was not over—not by a long shot—but the melting snow piles and warmer weather stopped the constant drifting of the existing snow on the ground, which had plagued snow removal for the majority of the winter. Snowplow and bulldozer drivers could, for once, work in tolerable conditions. High temperatures in the thirties and forties were by no means balmy, but they were downright tropical compared to the single-digit and below-zero temperatures, along with winds above thirty miles per hour, these men were used to working in.

Drivers could now see tangible progress in their work. Roads that had been cleared remained clear and did not fill back in with drifting snow. Nothing was more frustrating for a plow driver than to toil for hours on end, pushing snow out of the way, only to have the roads be closed again by a gusty wind storm, but the arrival of March brought new problems.

Melted snow signaled the arrival of mud and water puddles—and lots of them. Vehicles that struggled through snowdrifts in the months prior now got stuck in the muck and quagmire of muddy country roads. Sunken gravel throughfares with melting rows of snow piles running parallel on each side of them were transformed into virtual canals. What was worse: getting stuck in a dry, cold, snowdrift or in a wet, slimy mudhole? It was the ultimate pick your poison situation.

Although the snow melted slowly, some of the rivers in eastern Nebraska, such as the Elkhorn, Missouri, Loup, Platte and Big Blue, experienced some flooding. Much of the troubles along the Big Blue and the Platte Rivers were due to ice jams that formed in early February.[121] While flooding in northeast Nebraska was relatively mild for the amount of snow now melting in the above-freezing temperatures, the southern part of Nebraska, farther downstream, had more serious flooding conditions from the snowmelt.[122]

Seward experienced spring flooding in which the normally narrow river spread to be over two miles wide, rising two feet above its previous record high. Residents of Crete, national guardsmen and Doane college students dedicated their time to sandbagging efforts to try to prevent the Big Blue River from flooding the business district and the Fairmont Foods power plant.

Beatrice had a stream of water that cut right through its center. Water covered both the north–south and east–west bridges into town. To get from the south part of Beatrice to the main part, residents could either walk across the railway bridge or be ferried across on a big truck, which some had to use just to get to work. The Red Cross created a shelter at the Beatrice YMCA for those who had to leave their homes due to flooding.[123]

According to the *Lincoln Journal and Star*:

> *The Big Blue reached its highest stage in history at Seward and Crete, causing approximately 65 persons to flee their homes between Staplehurst and Wilber. Staplehurst Major Thomas Dahl said the river was a foot and a half higher than its 1913 peak and Seward County Sheriff Dick Dohrmann reported the river was six inches above the record crest of June 1948, at Seward.*[124]

Travel was impacted once again when powerful ice jams that could not be stopped along the Platte River took out several highway and railroad bridges. A bridge was washed out in an area near Linoma Beach along Highway 6 between Lincoln and Omaha. Those who wished to cross the Missouri River found it quite a challenge indeed. Not only was it difficult to cross the river, but its water also spread over hundreds of acres of farmland, turning the ground into a giant bog and blocking country roads.

Beemer and West Point had problems with the Elkhorn River overflowing, and the Middle Loup River crept across the bottomlands of central Nebraska.[125] After spending all that time snowbound, the people of Nebraska were now experiencing what it was like to be "mudbound."

While warmer temperatures brought ice jams and flooding to some areas, in other parts of Nebraska, the waterways tolerated the excess moisture quite well. The depth of the snow decreased, but it soaked nicely into the soil in most places. The melting snow in O'Neill did not seem to cause trouble, and the Union Pacific indicated that the streams in the Hoskins and Winside areas looked fine.[126]

The ice was expected to weaken and break up along the Elkhorn River, causing ice jams and flooding in some areas, but it was not expected to flood as badly as the Missouri or Big Blue Rivers. The Missouri River from Sioux City south was problematic, and the ice jams along the Platte River caused some flooding in Fremont, where water crossed Highway 77 just south of town, but it was not significant enough to stop traffic.

The Kearney area reported it was just fine. Ashland residents had some flooding from an ice jam along the Platte River that went into the Salt Creek, but it tapered off rather quickly. Their biggest problem was a chunk of ice that hit a gas line, causing twenty homes to be without gas until the line could be fixed.

Weather stations kept a close watch on area rivers as the ice began to break up. When the ice melted enough to start jamming up along the Elkhorn River near West Point, the river rose an entire foot within three hours. Some drainage systems could not work fast enough, which caused trouble in a few areas. Water flowed across Highway 275 between Wisner and Pilger and across Highway 77 in South Sioux City, Fremont and Lincoln. Pebble and Cuming Creeks, not far from West Point, were high and crossed country roads in places. Additionally, many gravel roads were too dangerous to use in northeast Nebraska, and it would take weeks, possibly months, before some would be in service again.

Travel by road was not the only type of transportation delayed when all the snow began to melt. As the Ponca Creek rose and water ran downhill, the railroad tracks in areas like Scribner, Verdel and Lynch were submerged. The Albion line, two miles west of Dodge, also had water over its tracks, and a line near Bradish reported water six to twelve inches deep over its tracks. More trains were delayed due to water reaching the tracks one mile east of Meadow Grove, where the creek bed was normally dry.

About five miles east of Lincoln, all train service was canceled due to damage to the bridge there. Although the rushing water did not wash away the structure, it had damaged about thirty feet of line on the west end, and the middle of the bridge was bent out of line. Another railroad bridge west of Linwood had two pilings damaged by the ice, but repairs were able to be made right away, and the trains were soon moving again.[127]

There was some water over the tracks near Beemer, Hoskins and Winside, but the worst of the damage to rail lines occurred just west of West Point, where six hundred feet of the Northwestern line were washed out. Trains could only operate from each end of the line and then go back again. If it had not been for the ice jams, the railroads probably would not have had any damage or disruption in service in the spring.[128]

Along the Platte River at Linoma Beach, not far from Ashland, two Creighton University students, Thomas Nolan and Charles Warmuth, went on a hunting trip Saturday morning, March 5, 1949, but soon they went missing. The river seemed low when they started out, but a dike broke upstream and caused the water to rise quickly, trapping the boys on a cramped island with water rushing all around them.

They did the best they could with what they had, which was not much. They had no food or shelter on their island, but they were able to get a fire started as they struggled to keep warm for the duration of the long night they had to spend there. The boys were unsure if the island would remain dry, so in the morning, they weighed their options.

Hungry and cold, Nolan and Warmuth decided they would wade through the icy river to try to reach high ground. When the water got waist deep, the two began questioning if they should be doing this. What if one or both of them was washed off their feet? The water was not running terribly fast, but it was ice-cold, and they would not be able to remain in it for long. They pushed on.

Determined not to turn back to the little island where there was no food or shelter, the boys plunged across the freezing water, even swimming at times, before they dragged themselves out and into the shelter of a game cabin about a mile from the island they had just left. Here, they were able to build a fire and dry out. They also found a couple of cans of soup, which was the first food either had eaten in thirty-two hours.

The following Monday, March 7, they left the cabin and found a canoe. The two were able to paddle their way to their car, which was right where they had left it on the highway, and they drove back to Omaha late Monday night. After spending a pretty rough couple of days on the flooded Platte River—thirty-two hours without food and fearing for their lives—Nolan and Warmuth had quite the story to tell when they were able to return to classes at Creighton University on Tuesday, March 8.[129]

Most of the flooding affected the lowlands. People along the Elkhorn River from Norfolk to Ewing were encouraged to evacuate and move livestock to higher ground. There was a lot of water in the Elkhorn River, close to its flood stage of ten feet, but the warming and melting trend did not continue.

With the weather dipping back down into below-freezing temperatures, the drainage along the Elkhorn River, as well as other Nebraska rivers, was able to keep up with the excess water and lessen the flooding situation. The ice jams were the cause of the majority of the flooding in lowlands, as was the water that flowed across the highways and railroad tracks. A few tenacious residents south of Norfolk attacked the ice jams with dynamite, hoping to divert the water into a new stream, but the river tended to do what it wanted to do.

While many of the rivers and streams in Nebraska flooded somewhat, it could have been much worse had the weather warmed more quickly. As it was, the warming and cooling off helped give the melting snow more time to seep into the soil. As is also common in Nebraska, cooler temperatures brought more snow to the panhandle. Scottsbluff and Sidney reported flurries, with about another inch of precipitation reported with the spring snow, but this did not make a lot of difference with the flooding situation.[130]

It was a wet and sloppy spring in 1949. Areas along the rivers and lowlands were surrounded by water due to all the melting snow. Residents would be working for many more months to drain all the water, repair bridges and rebuild washed-out roads, but miraculously, the flooding was minimal compared to how bad it could have been.

9

SOME MORE STORIES OF SURVIVAL

The best stories describing the historic snowstorms of 1948–49 were not those hammered out on newspaper scribes' traveling typewriters; instead, they were written with ink pens and whittled-down pencil stubs in letters to friends and family from those who actually experienced it. The following is a sampling of these letters from the *Lincoln Journal and Star*. From a letter by Mrs. George Manes, the wife of a flying service operator at Ainsworth, to her mother, Mrs. George Nye of Lincoln:

Dear Mom:

Will try to get a few lines to you tonight, tho I don't know if train service will get it to you. There is so much we have gone thru since Jan. 2, it seems like a horrible nightmare, but maybe I can give you some idea. I was almost out of my mind, and George is so thin his pants won't stay up. I did get him to the hospital for a checkup yesterday morning, and Dr. Lear says all he needs is lots of rest and a few regular meals.

For two or three days running no one here had anything to eat except what breakfast you took time to snatch about 5:30 a.m. We had to get up so early in order to get the pre-heater started to warm up the airplane engines so they would start by daylight. People were begging for help from daylight till dark and after, so we didn't take time for lunch, then when we got the hanger door shut at night, they were all so tired we would just go to bed rather than stay up long enough to eat.

It wouldn't have been quite so bad if the boys hadn't tried to fly in such bad weather and so late at night. One day the sun came out and warmed the snow up to the extent that they couldn't take off with the skis, it was so sticky. George had gone to Bassett to carry a doctor to a patient out in the hills, and just before dark he called and said he couldn't get off, and to send Don (Higgins an employee of the Manes) down with the Stinson, which we hadn't put skis on yet, and have him land on the highway and help him.

It got awfully dark and no sign of them. Finally, I got a glimpse of the navigation lights on the Stinson as it went down the runway and stepped to the door to watch. Just then the mechanic went sailing past and yelled, "They nosed her over!"

I told him to get to them as fast as he could. I couldn't look I was so scared. They catch on fire so easy when they nose over, and I expected to see it burning if I looked. After a few minutes I got my courage back and went out. I didn't know whether they were both in it or what to expect, but it was Don by himself and he got out all right, and it didn't burn. He said that after dark he made the mistake of landing on the wrong bare spot and hit a big drift. George came in about 20 minutes later.

On another occasion it was icing terribly, but George thought he had to go out in it to take care of someone. About dark I began stewing about him and stood by the window and strained my eyes in the last faint rays of daylight. It got darker and darker, and I just stood there and cried. It was such a mental strain on all of us, I don't see how we stood up under it for days on end. Finally, we called Rolland Harr of the department of aeronautics and told him we would have help in the line of airplanes and pilots. He sent up some help and even with three extra men we went all day long as fast as they could take off and land. It got to the place that we just couldn't hope to take care of all the calls, and people in their desperation began to get mad over the telephone. I can understand how they felt, but I just couldn't take that kind of treatment. Most of them were people who wouldn't give a tinker's damn about the aviation business until the time came when it was their only salvation.

I wish you could have witnessed those little airplanes, overloaded by about 300 pounds with food, feed, gasoline, fuel oil, coal, bouncing and weaving over that sea of drifts out on the field. They took a terrible beating, and it is miraculous that they are still flying. The people who were the most desperate for help lived in the most awful hills and inaccessible places. I have heard the men come in from a trip and make a remark such as, "My air speed showed 30 m.p.h. when I cleared those trees on take-off."

From notes written by Mrs. F.H. Frickey, the wife of a Burlington engineer:

Called at Sargent, Neb, Feb. 12 at 11 a.m. for trip to Aurora.

It was a doubleheader with wedge plow, as was snowing, blowing, and drifting when called. Made it thru from St. Paul to Palmer although hit heavy drifts. Were stalled between Central City and Marquette at 10 p.m.

Not being able to get out, the conductor started to walk to Marquette, a distance of two miles, to try to get in touch with Lincoln dispatchers to advise them of the situation as the water supply on both engines was getting dangerously low.

During the long hours of the night, they shoveled snow in the tanks. The crew remaining with the train were worried for fear the conductor had not reached Marquette. However, around daylight, he returned and had a few wieners and some sweet rolls from the Debus Bakery Delivery truck which was stalled, too. This was the only food they had.

The rotary snow plow rescued them at 2 p.m. Sunday and they were relieved at Aurora at 4:40 p.m.

The crew: Fred Frickey and William Koehn, Lincoln, engineers; Authur H. Wymore, Lincoln and Mr. Smith, Aurora, firemen; William Post, Aurora, conductor, and Glen Wright and Mr. Olsen, Aurora, brakemen.

From a letter written by Miss Carol Germany, Gordon, to W.F. Rumbaugh, Lincoln:

The storm struck like a cyclone the day I was 21 and not even a brave soul ventured out of shelter for three days. People were warned by telephone and radio not to even open their doors or go out into their own front yards. The fourth day a man came pounding on our door exhausted and lost to find that he was only a couple of doors from home, he had wandered about so he thought he was in another section of town.

When the 50 m.p.h. wind and blinding snow subsided we had to climb out of upstairs windows and dig tunnels from doorways to get out. Many drifts were as much as 20–25 feet high, completely covering some homes. Most families would not have tried to venture out even the fourth day had it not been that (being totally unprepared for this storm) they were running out of food. It was dangerous for older people to be out at all for the crust of a drift could so easily give way under one's weight and the drifts were mighty deep.

Then the second emergency set in. In a few days the stores' standing stock was exhausted and with no communications, they were not replenished. Fuel soon gave out and power lines broke down limiting electricity. From there on you can use your imagination as to the things that could happen when all communication and transportation is cut off. People who were out when the storm struck were either marooned at some shelter or froze to death, mostly the latter.

Here are some of the reports. A dear old lady friend of ours was found frozen to death in her home, evidently she had opened the door, as it was found open, and was unable to get it shut again. Furnaces blew up because the flues were clogged with snow and two of my Sunday school class girls burned to death.

From M.L. Booker, Bushnell:

We were unable to live in our house for several weeks because the snow drifts were higher than our chimney, and it took lots of scooping to keep the snow off the roof so it wouldn't cave in.

From Mrs. Cyril Richardson, Thedford:

We were fortunate not to lose any cattle during the storm. The cows, across the flat, had no hay from Sunday till Wednesday noon. There were drifts east from the house between 15 and 20 feet high, and now after two months, are still over my head, 5½ feet.

From Lloyd L. Lacy, Harrison:

The storm here was the worst ever. It started at 11 a.m. Sunday, Jan. 2, and lasted until the following Wednesday morning with no letup at all. Visibility was no more than 15 feet. With the severity of the storm, people in this community couldn't imagine stock of any kind living that were out in that storm. There was quite a loss in this territory and west of here but time will tell what the loss will be if we get another spring storm, leaving the stock in a weakened condition and a limited supply of hay and feed from the Jan. 2 storm.

We didn't have a train for 40 days and the highways were the same, as the wind and snow just kept blowing.[131]

A car drives in between two snowbanks three and a half miles south of Osmond. Travelers had a hard time reaching their destinations in 1949. *History Nebraska.*

The following is a letter that was sent to the *Colfax County Call* from Mr. and Mrs. Sylvester Shuster of San Francisco, who had come to Schuyler to attend the golden wedding anniversary of Mr. Shuster's parents. They were ahead of the storm on their way home to California until they reached Harrison, Nebraska.

Harrison, Nebr., Jan. 9, 1949

Dear Folks:

Guess you had our wire by now saying we were fine in spite of the blizzard we were in. It was quite an experience, enough to last us the rest of our lives. We'll always carry memories of it forever.

We left Gordon Sunday afternoon, and drove through Chadron and Crawford, the wind was blowing but not bad. Then six miles outside of Harrison it really caught us, just happened so fast, (the people here say this is a bad strip through here). If we had known it we could have stayed in the last town. It was snowing and blowing. It was 4:00 then. We were on the roads two hours longer trying to reach that town. Couldn't see a thing. Lots of others were all in the same shape.

Sylvester had to get the chains on, because the banks were getting deeper and deeper. (After the storm banks were as high as 30 feet.)

He got cold out there putting on the chains but we could smell something and thought it was the heater and defroster and shut that off, and our windshield froze over and we drove with the window rolled down.

Two couples piled into one car ahead of us, they had five children with them ranging from eight years old to a four-month old baby. Every time they got stuck in a bank we pushed them out as we had chains. Then their motor got wet and what a time we had.

Once we almost ran into them. We couldn't see them, so we passed them to break a track through for them and we kept watching for their head lights so that we knew they were still coming.

We were scared. I felt like crying but didn't. Instead, I prayed that we could find a ranch house to stay in. I guess God must have heard us, because just a mile from town, the other car got stalled again, and this time we couldn't push them out.

With our window rolled down, we heard a wind charger (that's what saved us). We said there must be a ranch house close to the road, but we couldn't see it. We found a white gate along the road, stopped the car, left the headlights on, and Sylvester went to look for the house. He found it locked, so broke out a panel on the wooden door and came after me. We took as many blankets, one small suitcase, all we could carry and started again. We crawled through several barbed wire fences and gates. I lost my overshoe and shoe in the snowbank but left it and kept on going and crawled through that panel. Don't ask me how we did it with so many heavy clothes on. It wasn't only six inches wide.

When we got in we found a circular heater, built a wood fire. Sylvester was all wet by this time, so he changed his clothes by the fire and started after the other people in the car. They didn't know we found the ranch house and planned to stay in the car all night but they would have frozen to death as the storm lasted too long, from Sunday till Wednesday noon. We got the back door open from the inside after we were in, and Sylvester helped carry the kids in, wrapped in blankets, as there was a 55-mile wind blowing. It was 6:00 when we got in the house and the temperature went down to 15 below. All eleven of us stayed in one room and put all the kids on the one bed, the grown-ups sat up sleeping, feeling lucky to be alive.

Oh yes! There was an oil transport from Gordon called Dillon Transport, Pat Nolan was in it. We asked him if he was going into Harrison or back to Crawford, as lots of people were turning back which was quite far and he said, "I'm headed for Harrison." He was so cheerful about the storm he said he knew the lay of the land and he'd find a ranch house or school house if he couldn't make it in, so he was following the second car behind us. Later he must have changed his mind because when they found him, he had turned the truck around and headed it back for Crawford. He had tried to make it to the straw stack and fell down and froze to death fifty feet from the truck. The truck was full of soot where he had been burning fuel oil to keep warm.

We were probably the last people to see him alive I imagine, and it upset us so, when we heard it Friday. The snow plow finally started through. Some men from town brought him back in a pickup. Sylvester saw him.

We had no phone, radio, no news from the outside world.

Paul had sent a ham with us and the other couple had eggs so we rationed out a slice of ham and one egg for all day during the storm and melted snow for drinking water.

The house was vacant, no people had lived in it for some time, but furniture was here. We were scared the owner would bawl us out for breaking in, but when the men walked into town for food, they found him running a dry goods store and he was so nice about it. He was glad the men had looked after the stock he has out here. He came in a pickup right behind the snow plow and brought us fuel. He said when the storm came he remembered he locked the door and felt bad because someone might need to get in.

The Coast Guard is dropping medicine every day and also nurses as there is no doctor in this town.

The baby is just fine, good thing it was a breast fed baby as there was no milk for it. The lady from this house came out from town and took the baby clothes in to be washed as they had been used and reused several times. Diapers I mean.

Today, Sunday, we are still here, as another storm came last night on top of the other. In fact the roads are still closed from the first storm. They have only ten miles from the Wyoming line but can't get there. After that they say they are open to Casper. These other nine people are all from Casper and so anxious to get home, so close and yet you can't make it.

They say at least 20 people were lost up and down the road between the two towns.

Today, Monday, the 10th we are still here. Fifty men went out today to break the road west of here. The town is out of food and fuel, and trains can't get through.

We got a copy of the town paper here in Harrison and Sylvester is quite the hero. He and the storm are on the front page. Guess he did his Boy Scout deed for that day.

Don't know when this will get mailed, as there is no mail service, but my letter will be ready to go whenever it is, so this news shouldn't be too ancient.

Two sick babies have been taken out of here by plane this morning, as I probably mentioned there is no doctor in this town.

I came down with the flu but am better now; had chills, fever, sore bones. Now the other lady has it. If we stay much longer, we will all be down with it. The other kids are coughing, but the baby is still fine, laughing and cooing.

The rancher is sure kind. He even brought out a radio so we catch the news and weather. Sure is cold, all the windows are froze up.[132]

10

LESSONS LEARNED
AND ACTIONS TAKEN

One of the first actions taken in the aftermath of the winter of 1948–49 was the improvement in the construction of roads in the state of Nebraska, be they rural gravel roads in the country or two-lane concrete highways. What made the blowing and drifting of snow so crippling was the fact that most roads in Nebraska were constructed flush or even below ground level, making them virtual trenches. This made it incredibly easy for blowing snow to fill in and pack the roads, making them impassable for vehicles.

Another factor was that the Department of Roads allowed weeds and underbrush to grow uncontrolled in ditches between the shoulders of the roads and the fields, which let massive amounts of snow accumulate during each subsequent snowfall. Worst of all, when snowplows did attempt to clear the roads, they created immense snow walls parallel to them, so it did not take any additional snowfall to refill the roads with snow, just a gentle breeze, making all the previous work for that section of the road pointless.

The obvious solution to this problem was to raise the levels of Nebraska's roads by a few feet and thoroughly mow the ditches that ran parallel to the highways during the spring, summer and fall so that blowing snow would not so easily accumulate in those areas. Beginning in the 1950s, and continuing today, along with constructing and maintaining adequate highways, the Department of Roads has been involved with roadside development projects and reducing soil erosion.

A light wind could blow snow onto previously plowed roads like this one, undoing earlier work. *Elkhorn Valley Museum.*

An effort is made to obtain a growth of vegetation on the highway shoulders, slopes, and roadsides to prevent wind and water erosion. Brome grass is sowed generally throughout the state and provides an excellent sod with ample root growth to materially assist in the prevention of erosion and to discourage the growth of weeds. Each year, the department harvests brome grass seed from the right-of-ways where good stands are available. During 1953, over 40,000 pounds of such seed were harvested and in 1954, over 65,000 pounds. Most of this seed is planted on recently constructed highways. Much improvement has been made not only in the appearance of the rights-of-way, but also the reduction of soil erosion.[133]

Even though World War II had been over for several years, there were still a great shortage of workers and materials needed for highway construction and maintenance, which hampered the modernization of Nebraska's roads. During World War II, railroads handled the lion's share (over 90 percent) of transporting people and materials across America to its coasts, where they were eventually loaded onto transport ships that would take them to the European and Pacific theaters of war.[134] So, naturally, the majority of workers involved in the transportation business in America, be they mechanics, engineers or construction workers, were employed by the railroads.

Also, during the war, around half of the men from the Nebraska Department of Roads either volunteered or were drafted into the U.S. armed forces or took better paying jobs in the private sector of wartime manufacturing, leaving the department very short-staffed. It was hoped that after the war concluded, the experienced men would return to the department, but that was not to be. The pay offered to Nebraska state workers simply could not compete with the pay offered by the private sector, thanks to the postwar economic boom. The result was a massive shortage of road construction workers who had the knowledge and experience to build and maintain highways.

As it happened, the State Department of Roads was saddled with a high turnover rate of workers after World War II. The state agency employed an average of 859 employees from 1941 to 1948. During that period, 1,375 employees left the department. But most devastating of all were the losses of engineering personnel, which was reduced by almost half after the beginning of the war. In 1941, 180 registered engineers were employed with the Bureau of Highways, and by the start of the road construction season in 1948, there were only 99.[135] It took years of training for new road construction workers and engineers to meet the demand of the postwar highway construction boom.

To fix this problem, the department created an expanded on-the-job training program, whereby chainmen were promoted to rodmen and rodmen were promoted to engineers and skilled maintenance men. It was a way to bypass the cost and inconvenience of college by creating the best of both worlds. Like workers in any apprenticeship, a chainman could work, get paid and get an education simultaneously, avoiding the pains of spending years as a typical broke, unemployed college student. This was of great interest to war veterans, especially those with no formal college education. The department went to great lengths to market itself to these men in particular. Slowly but surely, the Nebraska Department of Roads got its workforce back to prewar levels.

The other half of the problem was a shortage of raw materials, such as concrete, asphalt, steel and lumber, as well as snow-moving equipment, which was hard to come by and had inflated prices since it was being used overseas for the American war and postwar reconstruction effort. World War II also severely disrupted supply chains, allocating resources for wartime purposes instead of peacetime endeavors. It took years to get things back to normal. With the end of the war and the subsequent rebuilding of Europe, thanks to the Marshall Plan, surplus bulldozers, maintainers and plows were now available to be purchased by cities, counties and the state government of Nebraska in the early 1950s.[136]

Most important of all were the lessons learned by the hardworking veteran snowplow drivers and the knowledge that was passed on to new drivers who were learning their trade for the first time during that unforgettable winter. What worked for removing massive snowdrifts was recorded in manuals for future reference. What did not work was discarded. They learned by doing, and the best teacher for any activity is experience.

One other advancement was that of the methodology of weather forecasting. It took decades, but meteorologists slowly realized that the atmosphere behaves like a fluid, and its motions are governed by the same laws and principles of fluid motion and thermodynamics. By using those equations, meteorologists could begin to accurately model and predict weather patterns.

In 1946, the invention of the first electronic computer, the Electronic Numerical Integrator and Computer (ENIAC), and its first direct descendants revolutionized the science of weather forecasting. In April 1950, at New Jersey's Institute for Advanced Study, a group of scientists were able to produce the first weather forecast using both numeric prediction techniques and ENIAC as their tools. Even though their first forecast was only for a

Most cars at this time had only rear-wheel drive, making it very difficult to maneuver them on ice- or snow-covered roads. *Elkhorn Valley Museum.*

twenty-four-hour period and the computer calculations took more than a day to finish, the data produced was accurate. This marked the beginning of the numerical weather predictions we know today.[137]

> *The equations are so complex that supercomputers are required to solve them, for each grid point in three dimensions (horizontally and vertically); the higher the resolution (i.e., the closer the data points are), the more accurate the NWP models can become. Over the past 30 years, we've seen enormous advancements in atmospheric modeling techniques as a result of improved resolution, improved data sources (including satellite data), and improved physics/parameterizations (for example, mesoscale processes, ocean-atmosphere coupling, precipitation/ice microphysics, soil type/conditions, vegetation type/density, topography, and various heat/moisture fluxes just to name a few). As the models improved, the required computing power increased dramatically....Modern-day numerical weather models are run operationally on the NOAA/National Weather Service supercomputers in Maryland.*[138]

Supercomputers can now do quadrillions of calculations per second—quite an improvement from 1949.

CONCLUSION

I t was way overdue—the winter seemed to go on forever—but eventually, the spring thaw arrived. Events, such as basketball games, track meets, weddings and just run-of-the-mill gatherings of family and friends, were being held normally instead of being postponed or canceled altogether. The simple things in life, like driving the kids to school, getting to work on time and being able to buy the necessities, like food and fuel, became routine again. It is so easy to take the ability to do these things for granted in our rich and prosperous country, since we do them every day without a second thought. It often takes the shock of a natural disaster, like a blizzard, or the destruction wrought by a flood or a tornado to snap us out of our slumber.

One feature of bad winters in Nebraska—and the rest of the Midwest for that matter—is the lingering of big snowbanks in ditches and by fence lines long after winter has ended and the last snowfall has occurred. Even when temperatures soared into the sixties in March and April 1949, those snowbanks stubbornly refused to melt, but the most amazing reminder of that winter was the fact that patches of snow were still being found in tree groves on the Fourth of July. The densely packed trees of farmland shelter belts had provided such immense shade that sunlight was unable to melt the snow by midsummer. It was a stark reminder of just how severe the previous winter was.

The winter of 1948–49 has an enduring legacy in Nebraska, and the memories of it are forever branded on the minds of the people who lived through it. Imagine the near-death experiences of those who were stranded inside a car during a snowstorm and did not know if they would survive until the morning, the hunger pangs of not being able to get groceries for weeks or the painful lessons learned trying to keep livestock from freezing to death.

Just like the combat experiences of a war veteran, this event was never to be forgotten by the people who lived through it, and its memory was to be passed on to their children and grandchildren though the endless retelling of survival stories by the fireside, around dinner tables during family reunions or just in casual conversations from one person to another. From one generation to the next, the lessons of winter preparedness were pounded into children's heads. They were told to make sure to wear enough winter clothing when leaving the house, throw ice melt pellets onto steps and sidewalks before the arrival of an ice or snow storm to ensure no one slips and falls on the cement, winterize cars by late fall and use good-quality tires, have plenty of antifreeze in the engine, check to see if a good ice scraper is in the back seat and, last but not least, stay up to date on the latest weather forecast. Of course, the best course of action before and during a snowstorm is simply to play it safe and stay at home.

In addition to improving the physical conditions of everyday life, the end of that winter or any other winter for that matter is great for the mental health of an individual. I, the author, like many other people, am definitely a "feel like the weather is" type of person. Long stretches of cold weather, dry air and little sunlight are very depressing to me. On the other hand, when a warmup does happen, especially in the spring, I get an incredible sense of euphoria and well-being, an air of contentment that I just do not get when its cloudy and negative ten degrees, with a foot of snow on the ground. So, I cannot image the overwhelming joy the citizens of Nebraska felt when the winter finally ended in the spring of 1949. The sound of birds chirping and the sight of plants blooming and the grass changing from a dull brown to a lusty green must have been overpowering.

The summer of 1949 was an enjoyable, normal summer that Nebraskans relished as long as they could, but along with that was the nagging knowledge that winter would return again as it always did. It may not be as extreme as the previous winter, but it was still winter, with all the hardships that go along with it. But that is life in Nebraska.

The endless cycle of weather extremes from one part of the year to the next forces its people to adapt and adjust to whatever the atmosphere has in mind. It is forever reminding us that Mother Nature is in charge of things, not us. Planet Earth is our landlord, and we are its tenants, forever and for always.

NOTES

Chapter 1

1. Simmons, "Armistice Day Blizzard."
2. Robbins, "Brief History of Weather Forecasting."

Chapter 2

3. Dalstrom, "Never Going to Be Snowbound Again," 111.
4. Ibid., 112–13.
5. Ibid., 113–14.
6. "Pierce Tied Up," *Pierce County Leader.*
7. Ibid.
8. Ibid.
9. "Community Digs Out," *Pierce County Leader.*
10. Ibid.
11. Ibid.
12. Ibid.
13. Ibid.
14. Dalstrom, "Never Going to Be Snowbound Again," 114.
15. "Community Digs Out," *Pierce County Leader.*
16. Dalstrom, "Never Going to Be Snowbound Again," 114.

Chapter 3

17. Dalstrom, "Never Going to Be Snowbound Again," 117.
18. Ibid.
19. Winter, interview.
20. Dalstrom, "Never Going to Be Snowbound Again," 117.
21. Smith, "Oklahoma Blew Storm."
22. Ibid.
23. Ibid.
24. Ibid.
25. Ibid.
26. Ibid.
27. Cowan, "Deep Misery."
28. Ibid.
29. Ibid.
30. Phipps, "Outstate Editors."
31. Ibid.
32. "Snow Makes Big 'Headache,'" *Pierce County Leader*.
33. Ibid.
34. Ibid.
35. Mills, *Operation Snowbound*, 78.
36. Ibid., 31.
37. Ibid.
38. Coffey, "Great Job Born."
39. Ibid.
40. "Road Emergency," *Pierce County Leader*.
41. Coffey, "Great Job Born."
42. "Snow Drifts and Ice," *Pierce County Leader*.
43. Ibid.
44. Ibid.
45. Coffey, "Great Job Born."

Chapter 4

46. Dalstrom, "Never Going to Be Snowbound Again," 137.
47. Coffey, "Great Job Born."
48. Ibid.
49. Ibid.

50. Dalstrom, "Never Going to Be Snowbound Again," 140.
51. Ibid., 141.
52. Mills, *Operation Snowbound*, 24.
53. Ibid., 24–25.
54. Dalstrom, "Never Going to Be Snowbound Again," 146.
55. Ibid.
56. Baudouin, "Weasel M29."
57. Dalstrom, "Never Going to Be Snowbound Again," 142.
58. Nash, "Cargo Carrier M29 Weasel."
59. Dalstrom, "Never Going to Be Snowbound Again," 128.
60. "'Mercy' Missions," *Pierce County Leader*.
61. Dalstrom, "Never Going to Be Snowbound Again," 143.
62. Ibid., 148.
63. Mills, *Operation Snowbound*, 67.
64. "Opening Progresses Slowly," *Pierce County Leader*.
65. Ibid.
66. Coffey, "Great Job Born."
67. Dalstrom, "Never Going to Be Snowbound Again," 148.
68. Coffey, "Great Job Born."
69. Ibid.
70. Ibid.
71. Ibid.
72. Ibid.
73. "Chronological Highlights," *Omaha World-Herald*.
74. Smith, "Struggle to Escape."
75. Ibid.
76. Ibid.
77. Ibid.
78. Williams, "70 Inches Deep.'"
79. Dalstrom, "Never Going to Be Snowbound Again," 139.
80. Williams, "70 Inches Deep.'"
81. Dalstrom, "Never Going to Be Snowbound Again," 139.
82. Williams, "70 Inches Deep.'"
83. Ibid.
84. Ibid.
85. "Verdel Family," *Lincoln Sunday Journal and Star*.
86. "There Was a Lighter Side," *Lincoln Sunday Journal and Star*.
87. "Verdel Family," *Lincoln Sunday Journal and Star*.
88. Matzke, "Farmers Wanted No More."

89. Ibid.

90. Ibid.

91. "Problem Was to Find Highways," *Lincoln Sunday Journal and Star.*

92. Matzke, "Farmers Wanted No More."

93. Ibid.

94. Ibid.

95. "Problem Was to Find Highways," *Lincoln Sunday Journal and Star.*

96. Ibid.

97. "There Was a Lighter Side," *Lincoln Sunday Journal and Star.*

Chapter 5

98. Koffend, "Top Honors for Henriette."

99. Ibid.

100. Ibid.

101. Dalstrom, "Never Going to Be Snowbound Again," 146.

102. Ibid., 147.

103. Ibid.

Chapter 6

104. Smith, "Oklahoma Blew Storm."

105. "Jones Was Just Another Rounder," *Lincoln Sunday Journal and Star.*

106. Ibid.

107. Ibid.

108. Ibid.

109. Mills, *Operation Snowbound*, 168.

110. Ibid., 169–70.

111. "Seeing Was Believing," *Lincoln Sunday Journal and Star.*

112. Dalstrom, "Never Going to Be Snowbound Again," 117.

113. Ibid., 118.

114. Ibid.

115. Alleman, *Blizzard*, 35.

116. Ibid., 36–41.

Chapter 7

117. Dalstrom, "Never Going to Be Snowbound Again," 117.
118. Robinson, "Winter Survival Skills."
119. Dalstrom, "Never Going to Be Snowbound Again," 133.
120. "Emergency Over," *Pierce County Leader*.

Chapter 8

121. "Aftermath," *Lincoln Sunday Journal and Star*.
122. "Blue River Flood," *Norfolk Daily News*.
123. Ibid.
124. "Aftermath," *Lincoln Sunday Journal and Star*.
125. Ibid.
126. "Ice Breakup Is Expected," *Norfolk Daily News*.
127. "Ice Gorges," *Norfolk Daily News*.
128. "Water Rips Out 600 Feet," *Norfolk Daily News*.
129. "Students Swim," *Norfolk Daily News*.
130. "Elkhorn Is Likely to Flood," *Norfolk Daily News*.

Chapter 9

131. "Seeing Was Believing," *Lincoln Sunday Journal and Star*.
132. "Pat Knew the Lay of the Land," *Pierce County Leader*.

Chapter 10

133. Koster, "Story of Highway Development," 58.
134. Ibid., 49.
135. Ibid., 50.
136. Ibid., 50, 55.
137. Robbins, "Brief History of Weather Forecasting."
138. Ibid.

BIBLIOGRAPHY

Alleman, Roy V. *Blizzard: 1949*. Grand Island, NE: NebraskaWealth.org, 1991.

Baudouin, Aurélien. "The Weasel M29, a WWII All-Terrain Vehicle." Normandy Victory Museum. July 28, 2021. https://normandy-victory-museum.fr/en/the-weasel-m29-a-wwii-all-terrain-vehicle.

Coffey, Max. "A Great Job Born of Necessity." *Omaha World-Herald*, January 1949. Special edition.

Cowan, J. Harold. "Deep Misery for Man with Mile-Wide Appetite." *Omaha World-Herald*, January 1949. Special edition.

Dalstrom, Harl A. "I'm Never Going to Be Snowbound Again: The Winter of 1948–1949 in Nebraska." *Nebraska History* 82 (Fall/Winter 2002): 110–66.

Koffend, John. "Top Honors for Henriette—And a Weasel Named Flo.'" *Omaha World-Herald*, January 1949. Special edition.

Koster, George E. "A Story of Highway Development in Nebraska." Department of Roads: Lincoln, Nebraska. Last modified 1997. https://dot.nebraska.gov/media/1205/history-general.pdf.

Lincoln Sunday Journal and Star. "Aftermath—Icy Rivers Overflowed." April 1949. Blizzard of 1949 edition.

———. "Casey Jones Was Just Another Rounder as New Rail Legends Were Born." April 1949. Blizzard of 1949 edition.

———. "The Problem Was to Find Highways." April 1949. Blizzard of 1949 edition.

———. "Seeing Was Believing—These Victims Saw What Hit 'Em." April 1949. Blizzard of 1949 edition.

———. "There Was a Lighter Side, Too." April 1949. Blizzard of 1949 edition.

———. "Verdel Family Refused Rescue to Save Cows." April 1949. Blizzard of 1949 edition.

Matzke, Stanley. "Farmers Wanted No More, But Blizzards of 1949 Were 'Great Experience.'" *Lincoln Sunday Journal and Star*, April 1949. Blizzard of 1949 edition.

Mills, David W. *Operation Snowbound: Life Behind the Blizzards of 1949*. Fargo: North Dakota State University Press, 2018.

Nash, Mark. "Cargo Carrier M29 Weasel." Tank Encyclopedia. July 25, 2017. https://tanks-encyclopedia.com/ww2/us/cargo-carrier-m29-weasel.

Norfolk Daily News. "Blue River Flood Bisects Beatrice." March 8, 1949.

———. "Elkhorn Is Likely to Flood Lowland from Ewing to Norfolk." March 8, 1949.

———. "High Water Rips Out 600 Feet of C.&N.W. Track at West Point." March 7, 1949.

———. "Ice Breakup Is Expected Near Here in 48 Hours." March 4, 1949.

———. "Ice Gorges Start to Form in This Region." March 5, 1949.

———. "Students Swim Through Flood." March 8, 1949.

Omaha World-Herald. "Chronological Highlights of State's Worst Storms." January 1949. Special edition.

Phipps, Robert. "Outstate Editors Growled or Laughed at Storm." *Omaha World-Herald*, January 1949. Special edition.

Pierce County Leader. "Emergency Over in the South Half of County." February 17, 1949.

———. "How One Community Digs Out." January 13, 1949.

———. "Pat Knew the Lay of the Land but He Froze to Death in the Storm." January 27, 1949.

———. "Pierce Tied Up by First Blizzard." November 25, 1948.

———. "Road Emergency." January 20, 1949.

———. "Road Opening Progresses Slowly as Snow Drifts." February 10, 1949.

———. "Snow Drifts and Ice Block Roads All Plows Working 24 Hours Per Day." February 3, 1949.

———. "Snow Makes Big 'Headache' for State and County Officers." January 20, 1949.

———. "Weasels Make 'Mercy' Missions." February 17, 1949.

Robbins, Chris. "A Brief History of Weather Forecasting." iWeathernet. com. January 17, 2015. https://www.iweathernet.com/educational/ history-weather-forecasting.

Robinson, Tammy. "Winter Survival Skills That Kept the Pioneers Alive." *Off the Grid News*, January 11, 2018. https://www.offthegridnews.com/ lost-ways-found/winter-survival-skills-that-kept-the-pioneers-alive.

Simmons, Theresa. "Armistice Day Blizzard of 1940 Remembered." National Weather Service. https://www.weather.gov/dvn/armistice_ day_blizzard.

Smith, Ralph. "Oklahoma Blew Storm Our Way." *Omaha World-Herald*, January 1949. Special edition.

————. "Struggle to Escape Storm's Grip Seen from the Air." *Omaha World-Herald*, January 1949. Special edition.

Williams, Paul. "70 Inches Deep—'Haven't Missed a Single Blizzard.'" *Omaha World-Herald*, January 1949. Special edition.

Winter, JoAnn. Interview with the author. October 2022.

ABOUT THE AUTHOR

Nebraska native Barry D. Seegebarth is a lifelong citizen of eastern Nebraska, an avid reader and a history buff. He currently lives with his wife in northeast Nebraska.